A Step by Step Guide
CogAT – Form 7
(Cognitive Abilities Test)

NUMBER PUZZLES

Grade 2
By MindMine

Find out what number should replace the question mark to make the equation correct?

✡✡✡✡ ✡✡✡✡	=	✡✡	+	?

CONCEPT:

- **Number Puzzles are finding the missing number that balances one side of an equation with another side.**
- **What is on the LEFT, MUST equal to what is on the RIGHT**
- **Solve in One-Step, Two-Step or Multi-Step**

NUMBER PUZZLES

in

PICTURE FORMAT

One-Step Equations

ADDITION

LEFT Side **RIGHT Side**

$= \quad + \quad ?$

MATH WAY						
STEP#1	Count pictures on BOTH sides	9	=	6	+	?
STEP#2	Solve ADDITION on RIGHT SIDE	9	=	6	+	**3**
ANSWER						**3**

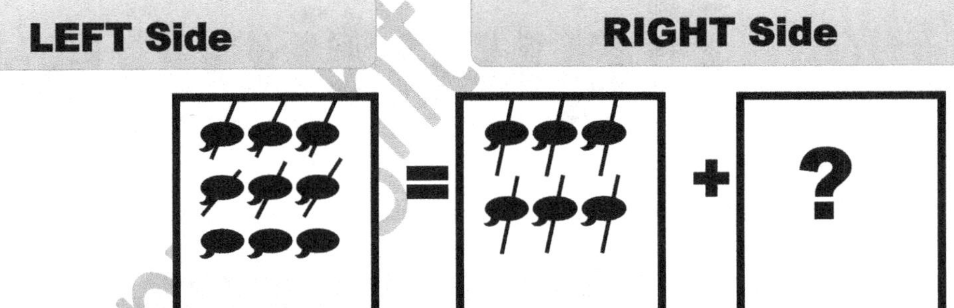

COUNTING TECHNIQUE						
STEP#1	Count pictures on RIGHT side. Strike out as you count			6		?
STEP#2	Strike out same number of pictures on LEFT side	6				
STEP#3	Count REMAINING pictures on LEFT side	3				
ANSWER						3

Tip: If you see SAME Number with Same Sign on both sides of Equal sign (=), Simply strike out (Eliminate from equation)

$$5 + \cancel{2} = 3 + \cancel{2} + ?$$

Question 1

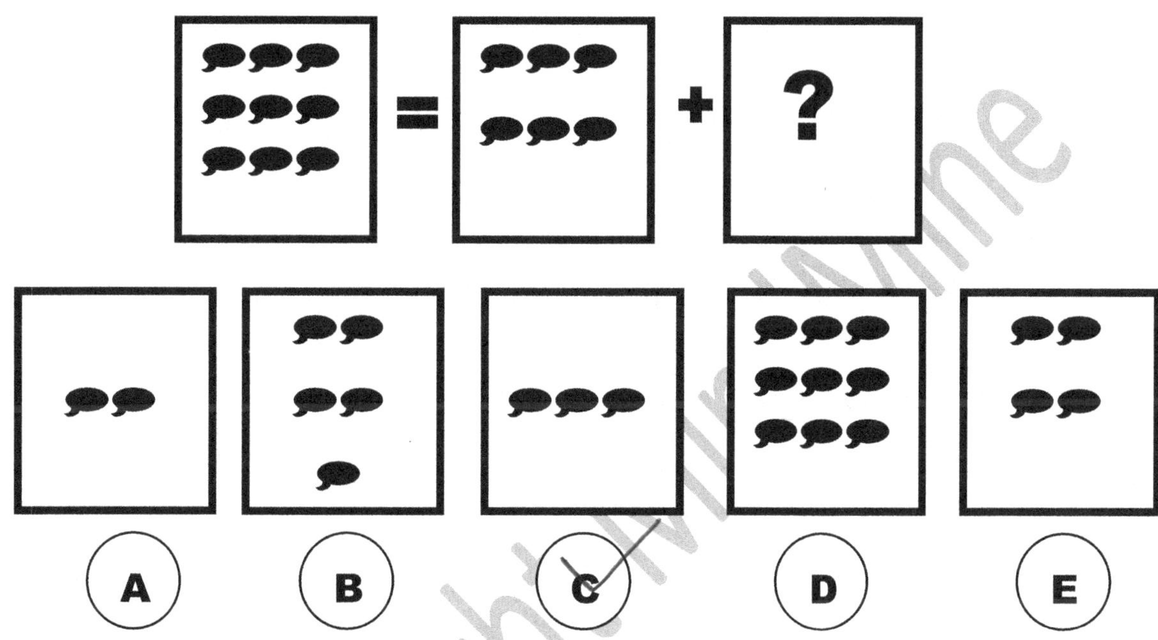

Question 2

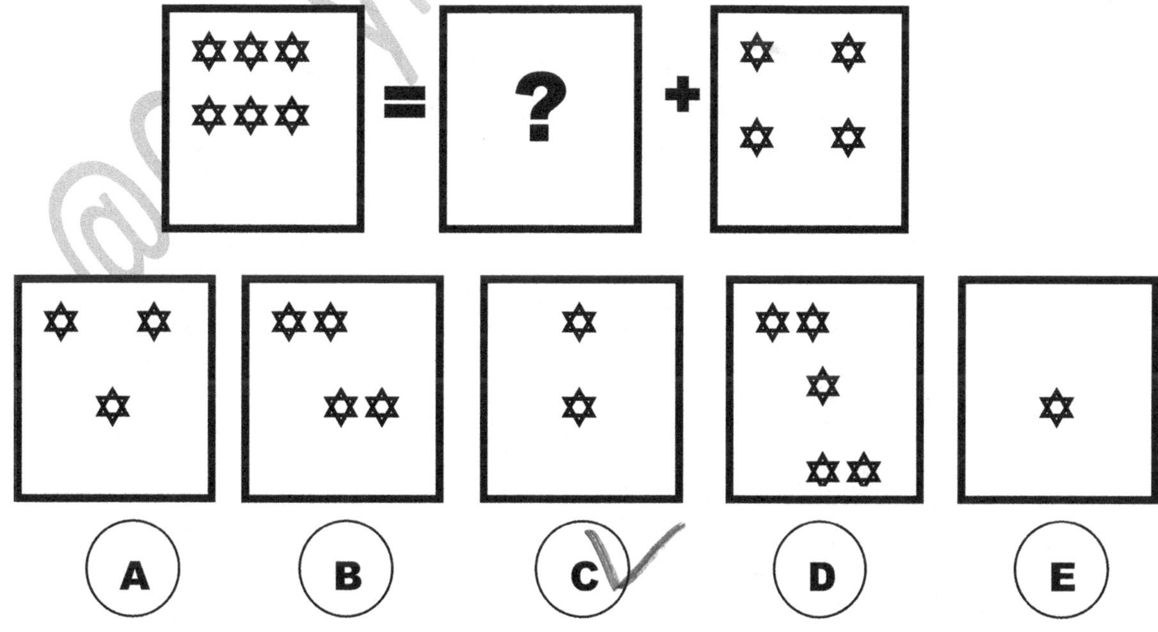

Question 3

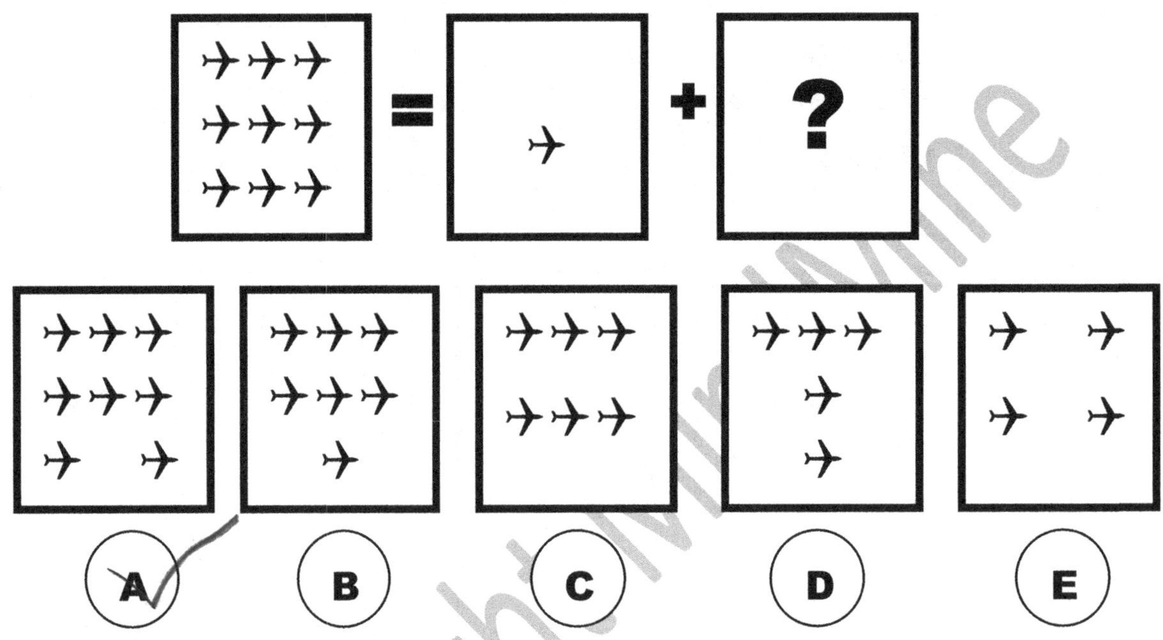

Question 4

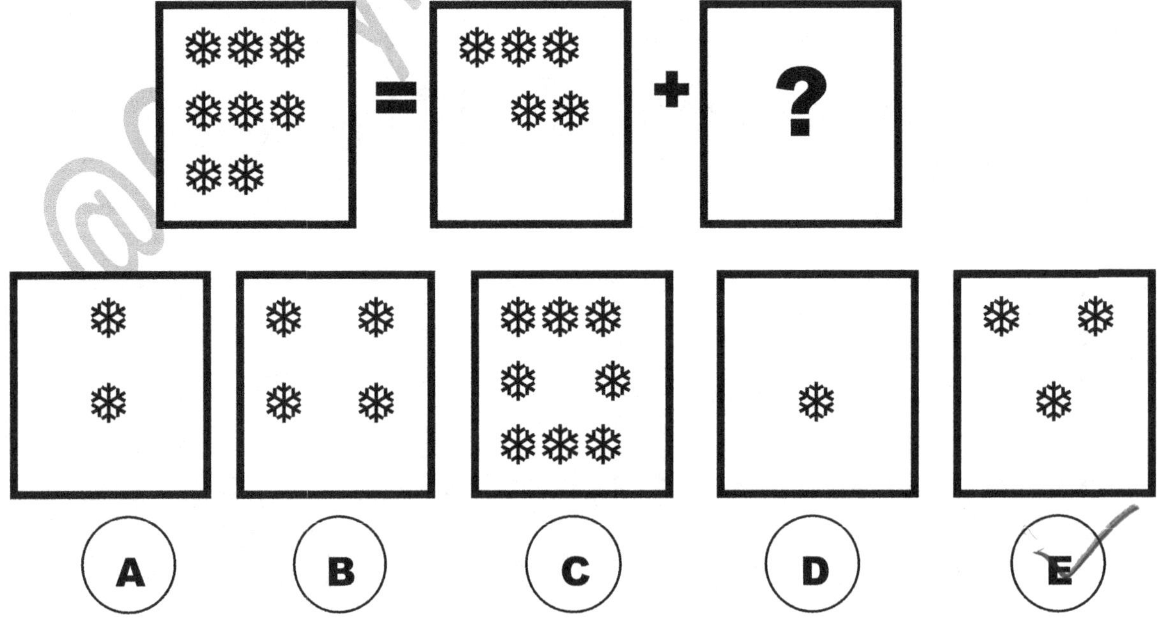

Question 5

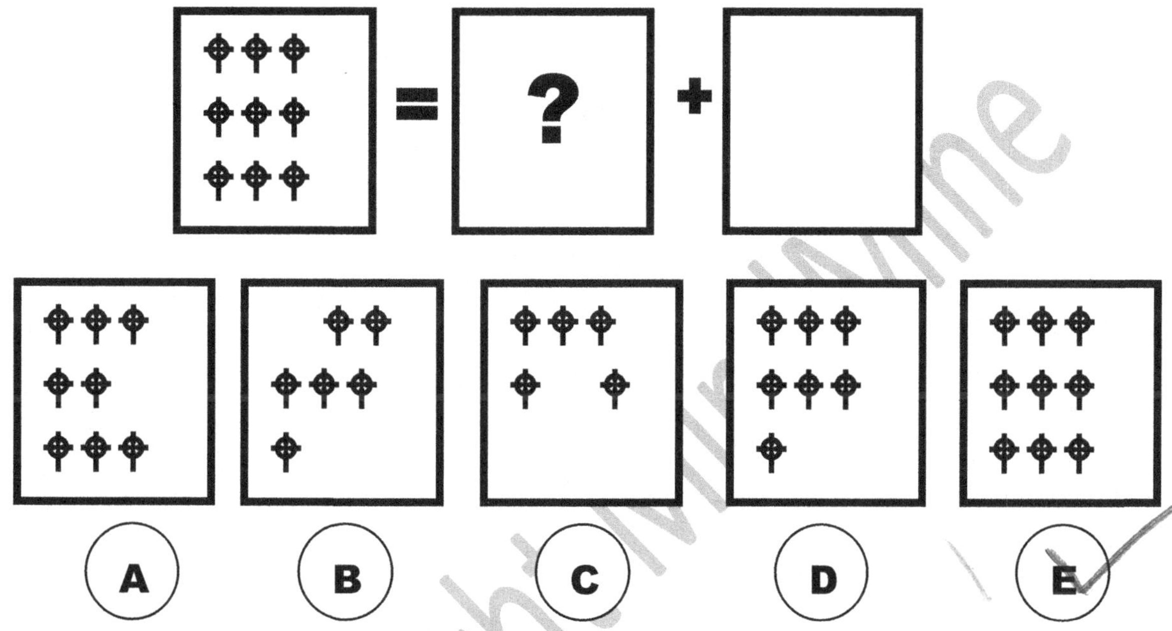

Question 6

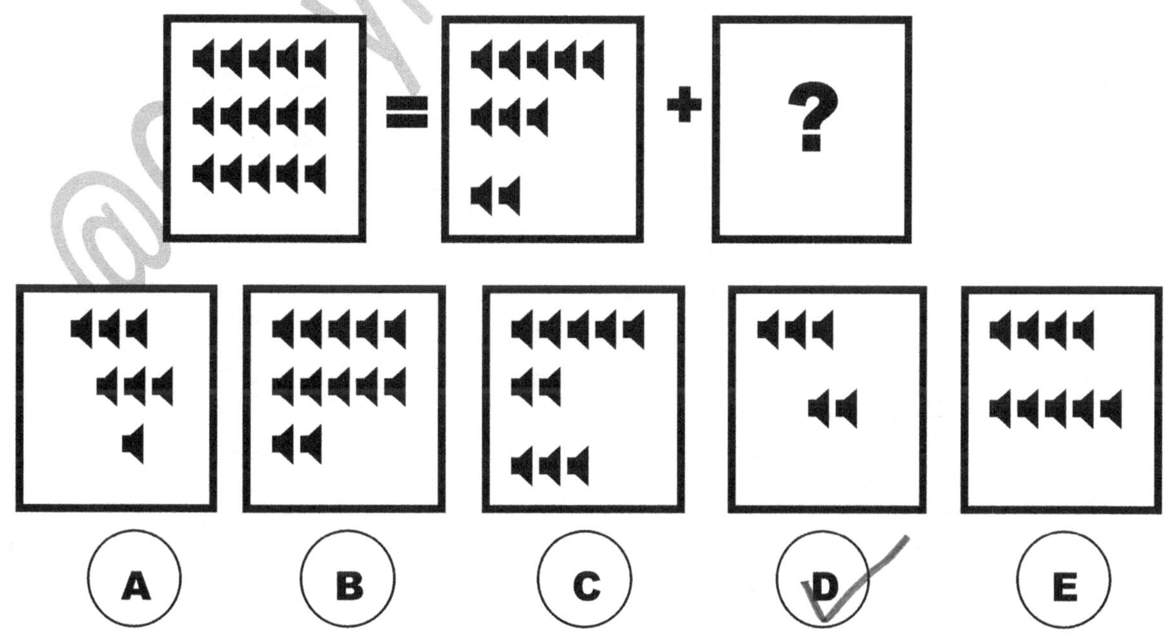

Question 7

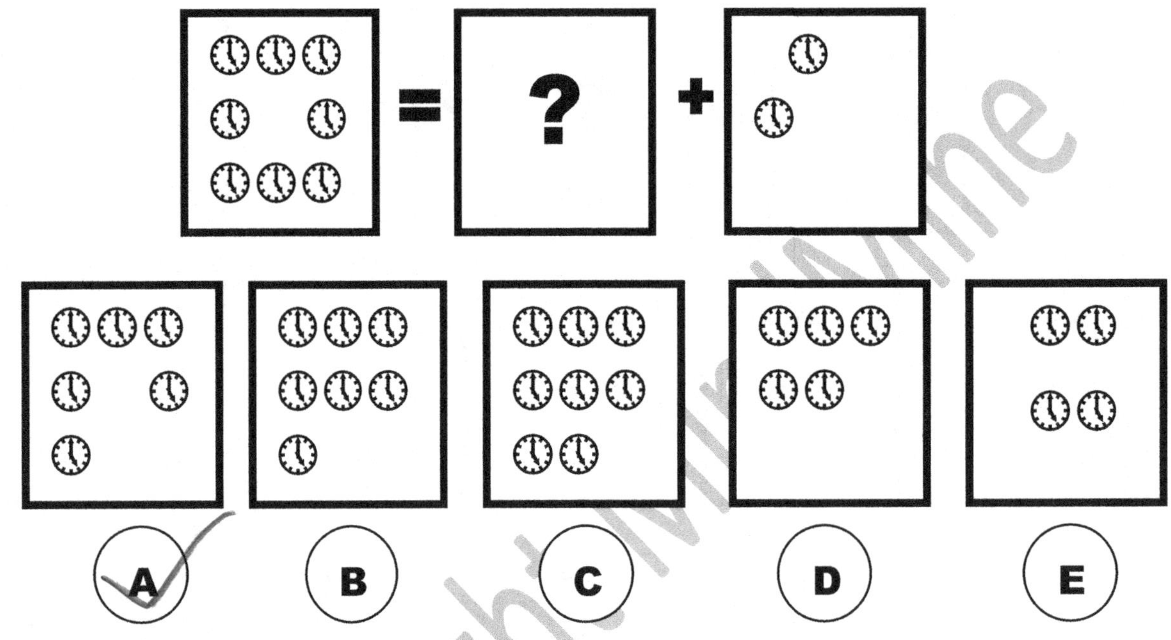

Question 8

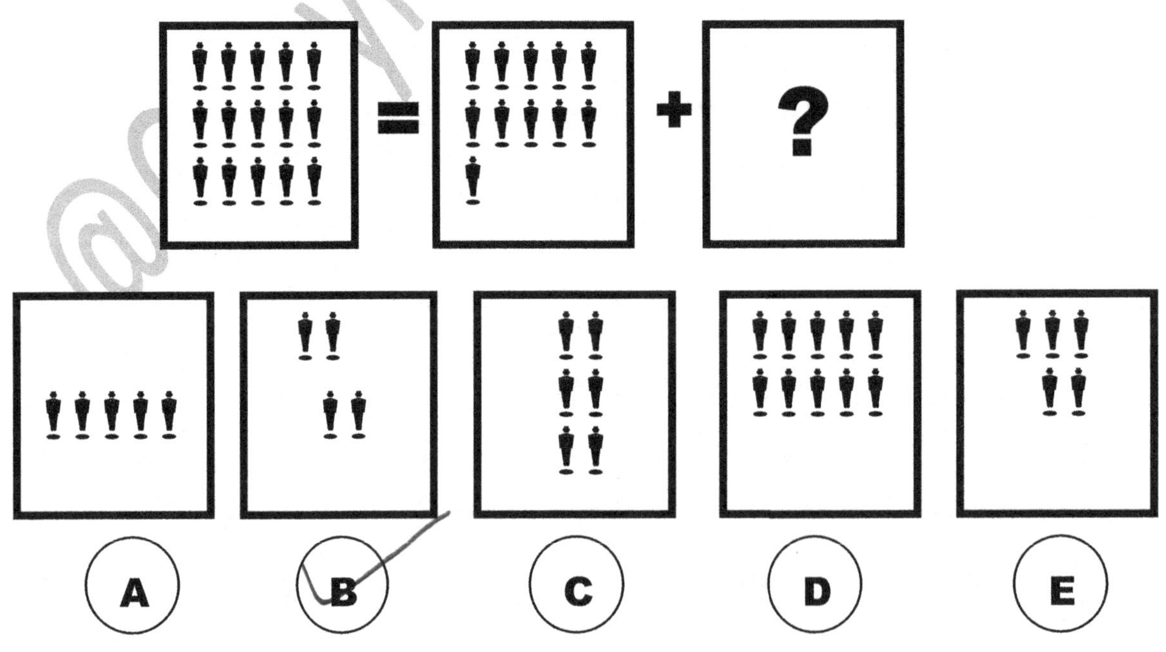

Question 9

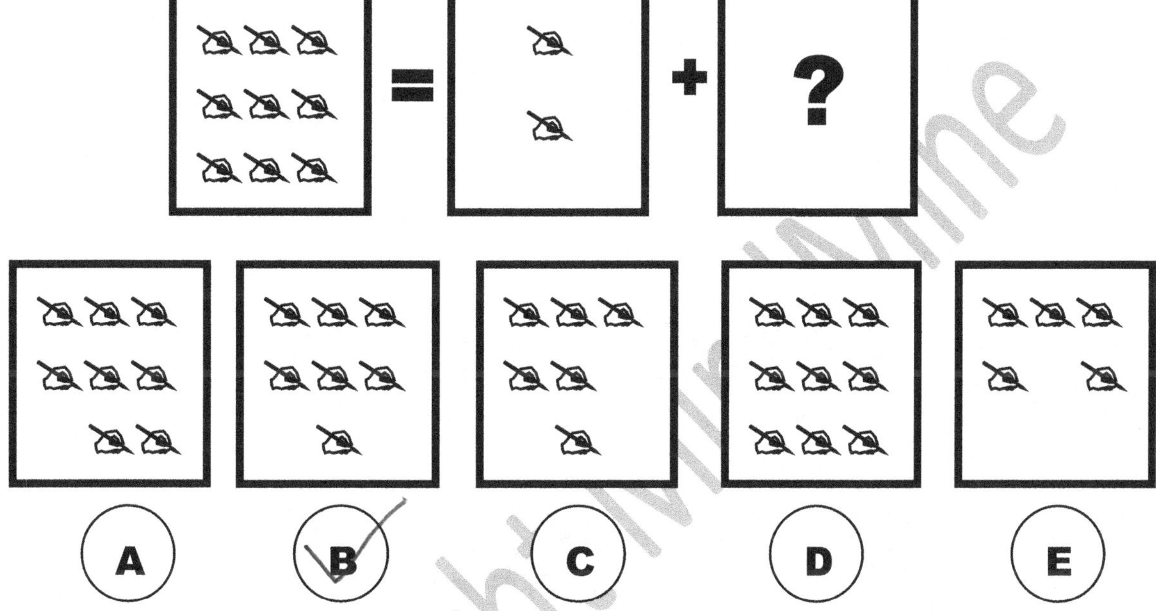

Question 10

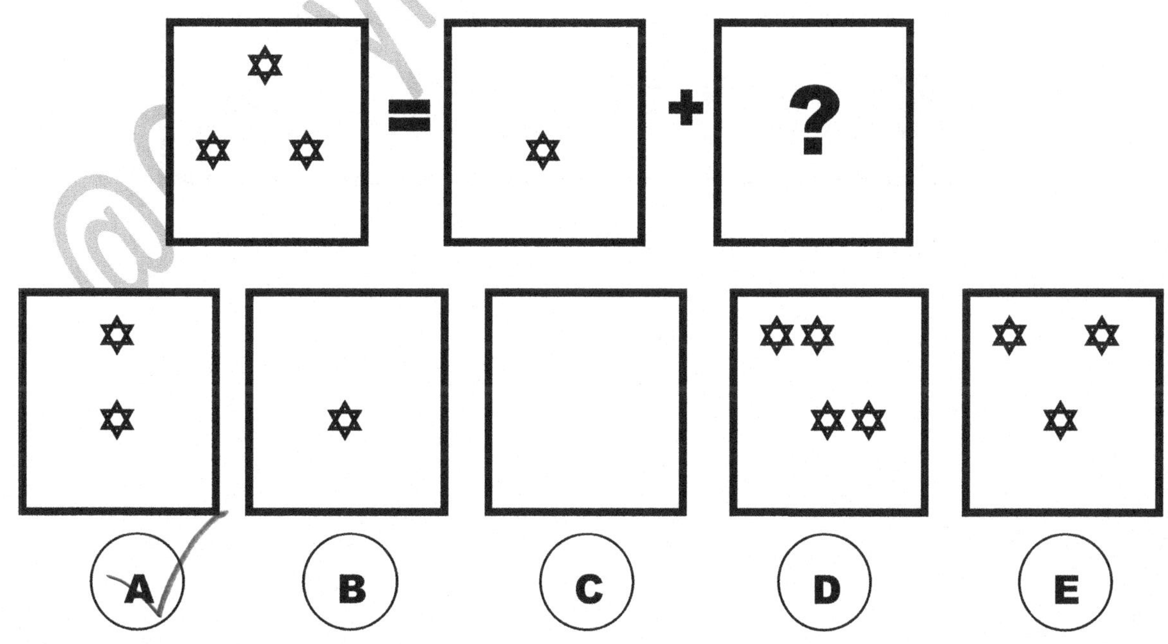

One-Step Equations

SUBTRACTION

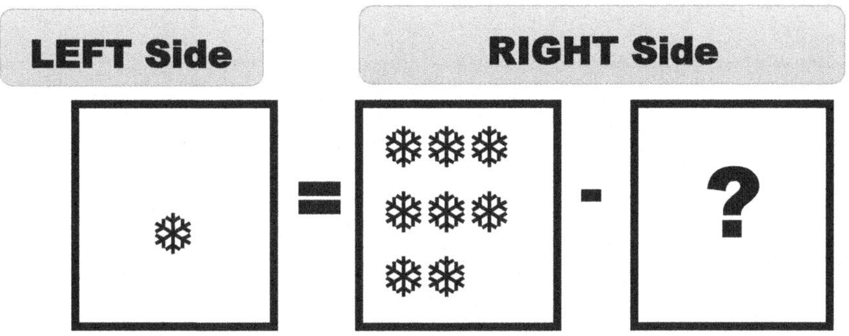

MATH WAY						
STEP#1	Count pictures on BOTH sides	1	=	8	-	?
STEP#2	Solve SUBTRACTION on RIGHT side	1	=	8	-	7
ANSWER					7	

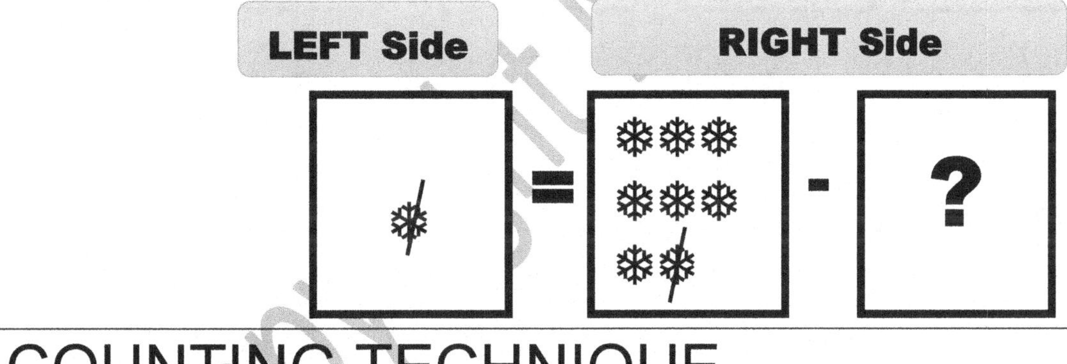

COUNTING TECHNIQUE						
STEP#1	Count pictures on LEFT side. Strike out as you count	1				
STEP#2	Strike out SAME number of pictures on RIGHT SIDE			1		
STEP#3	Count REMAINING pictures on RIGHT side			7		
ANSWER						7

NOTE: Will NOT work if question mark is in the middle box

Tip: If you see SAME Number with Same Sign on both sides of Equal sign (=), Simply strike out (Eliminate from equation)

5 - ~~2~~ = 3 - ~~2~~ + ?

Question 1

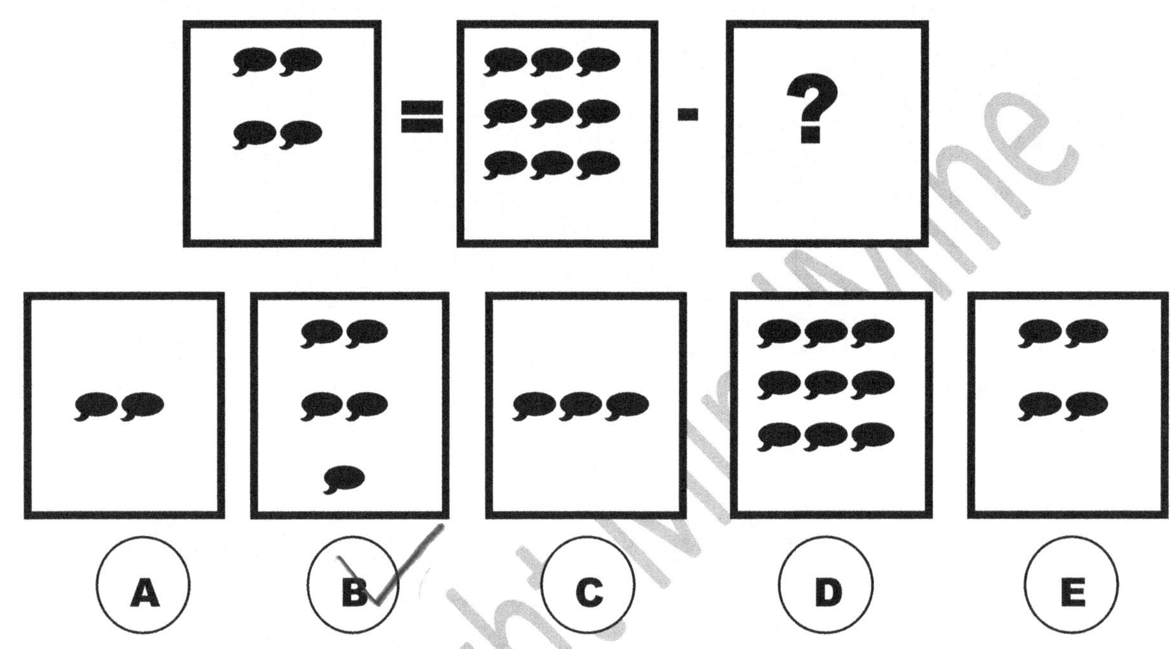

Question 2

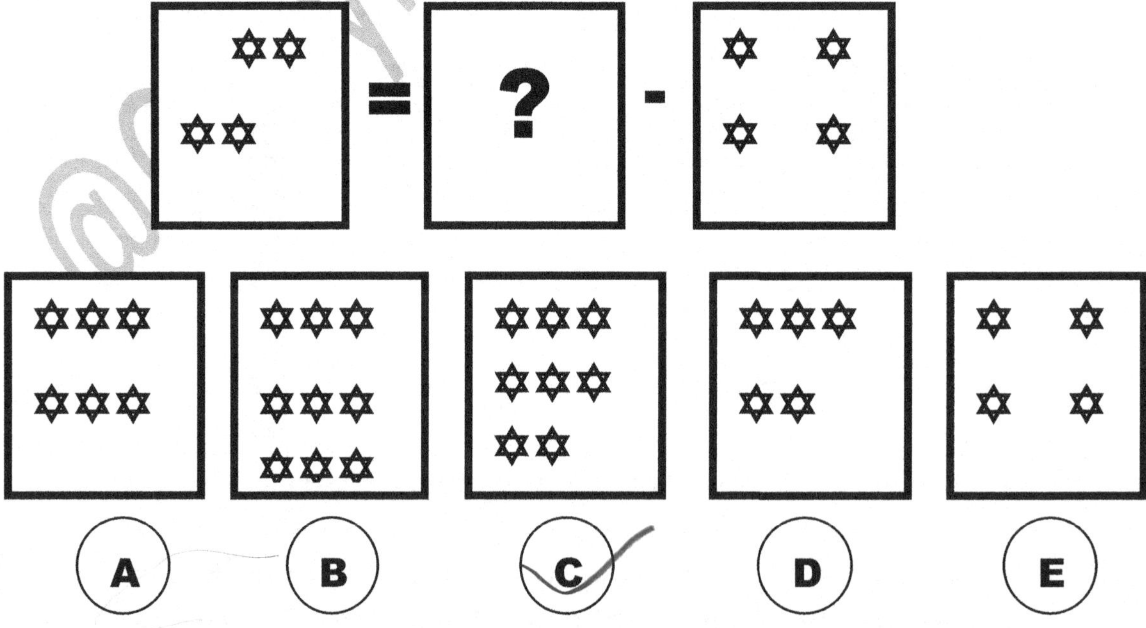

Question 3

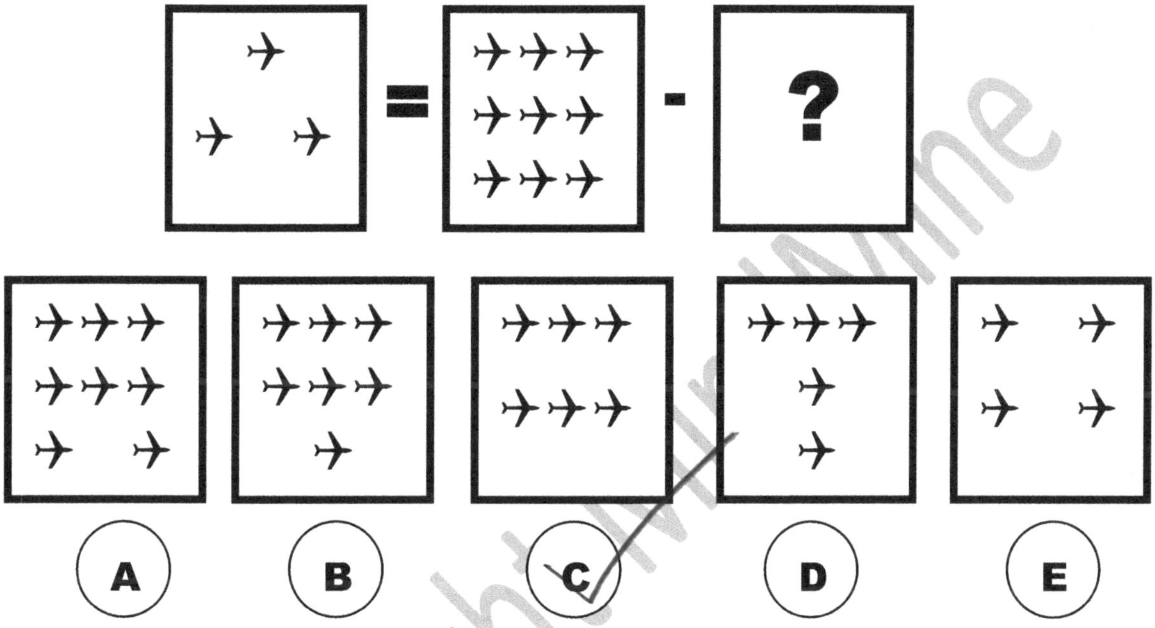

A B C D E

Question 4

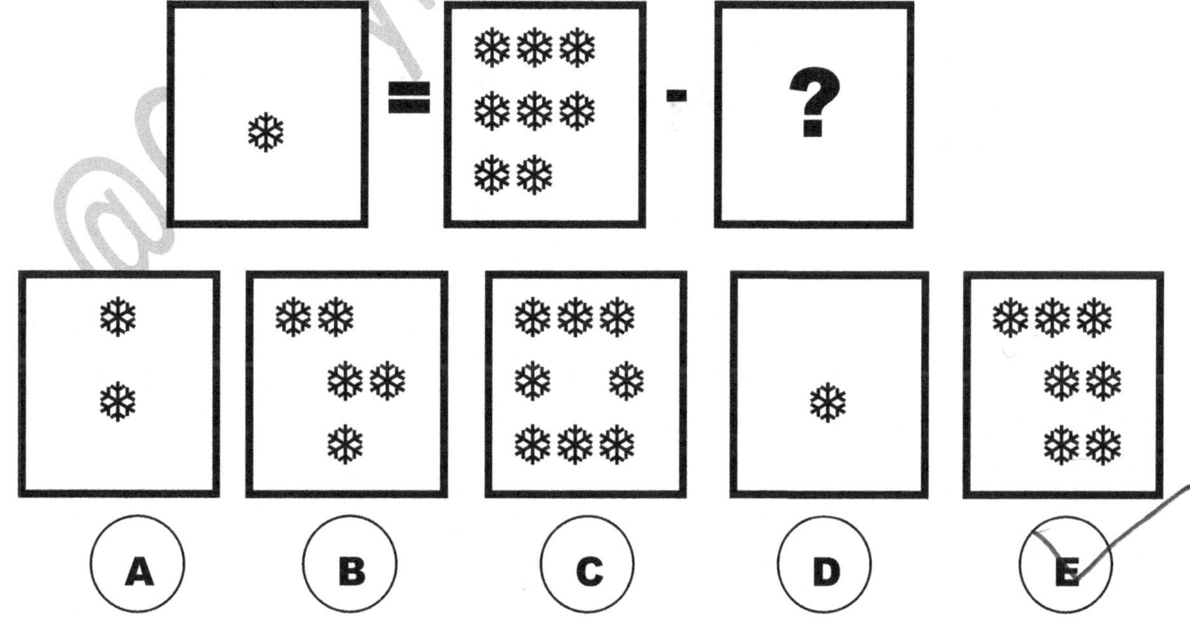

Question 5

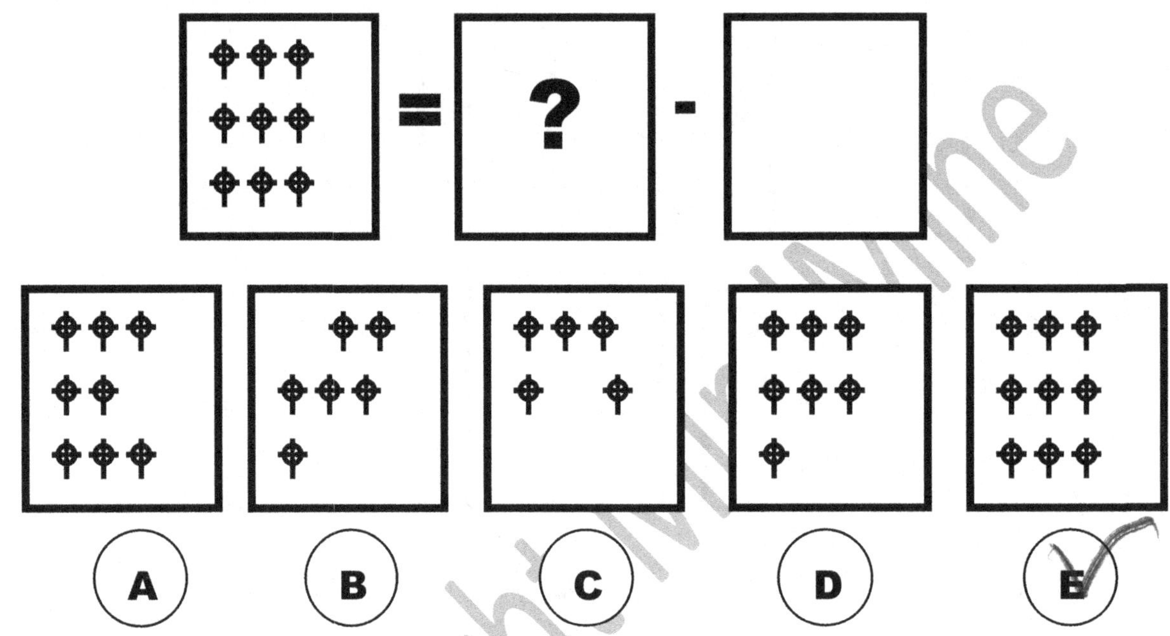

Question 6

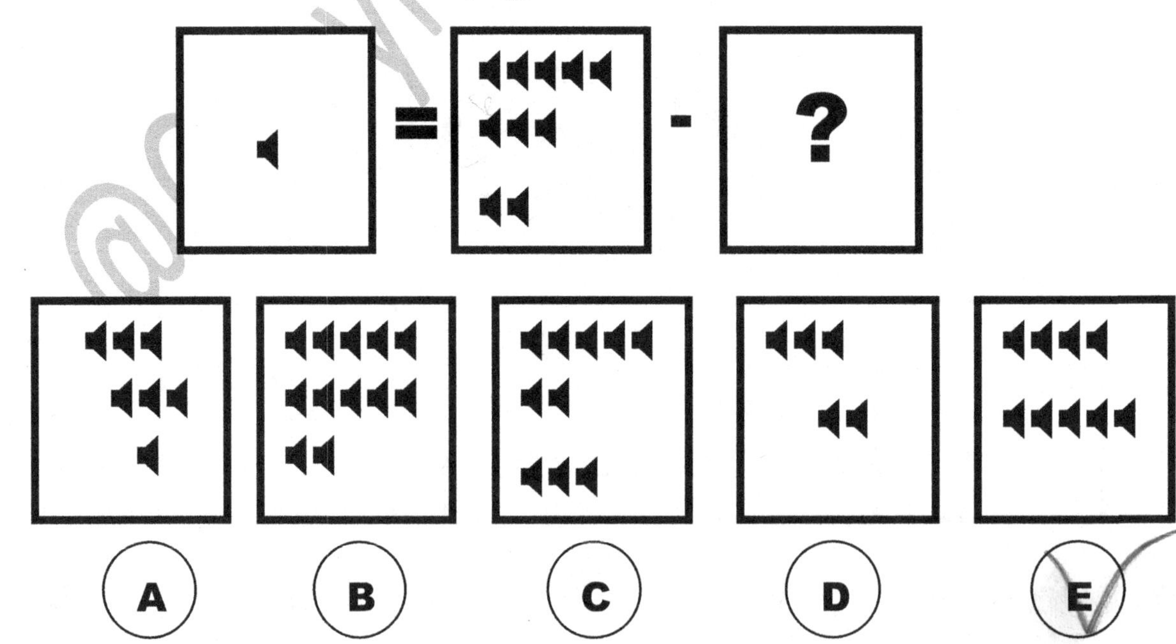

Question 7

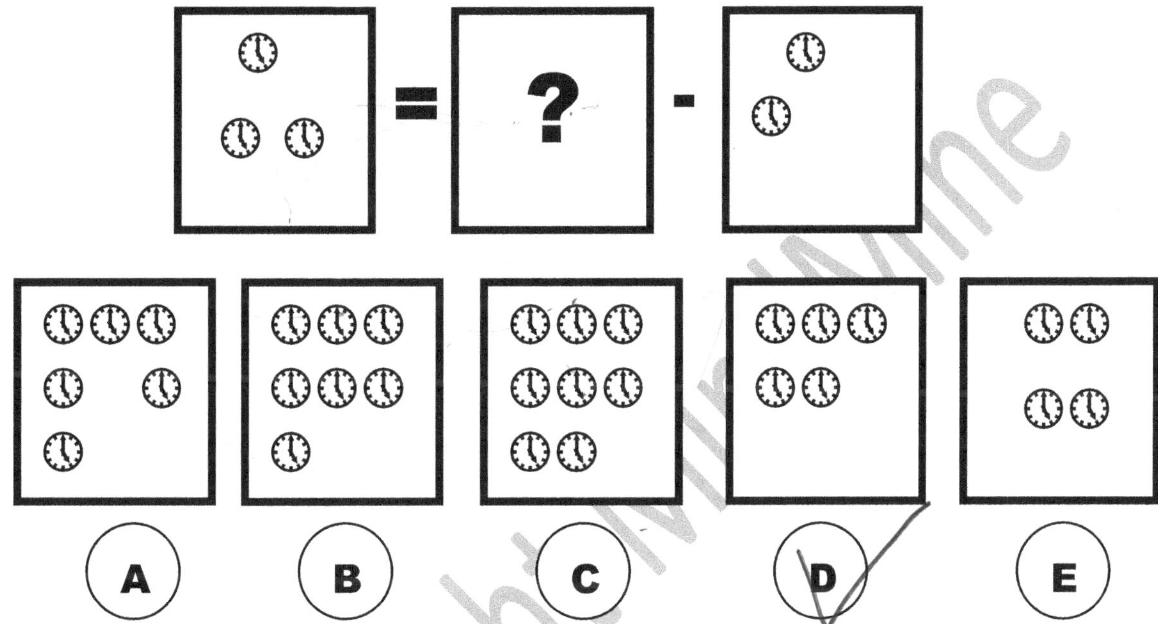

Question 8

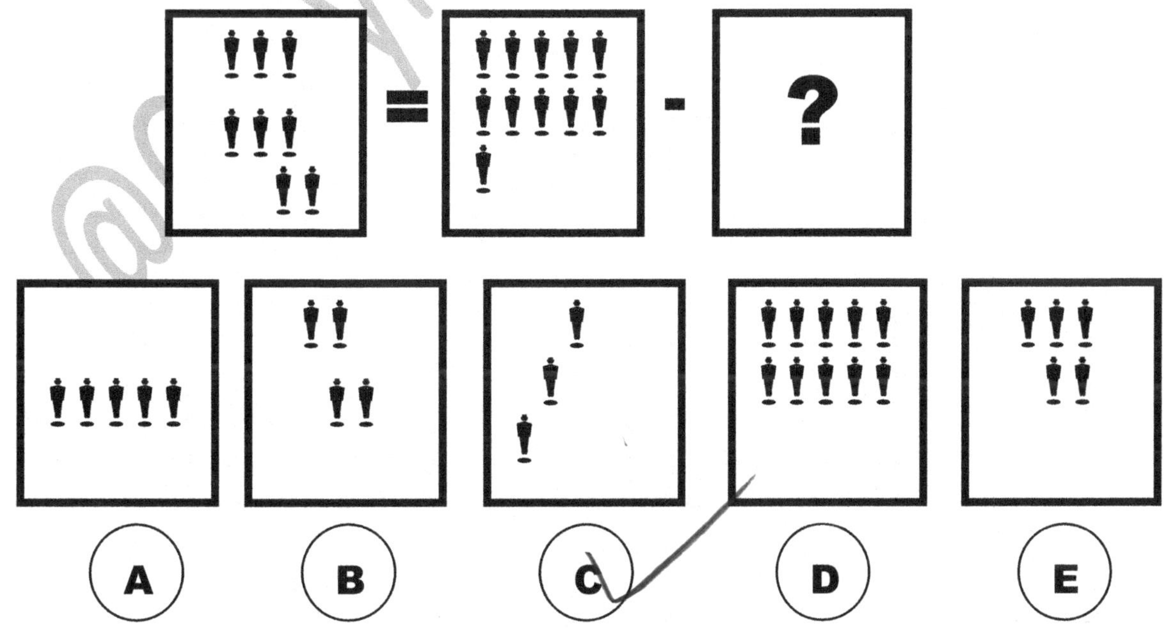

Question 9

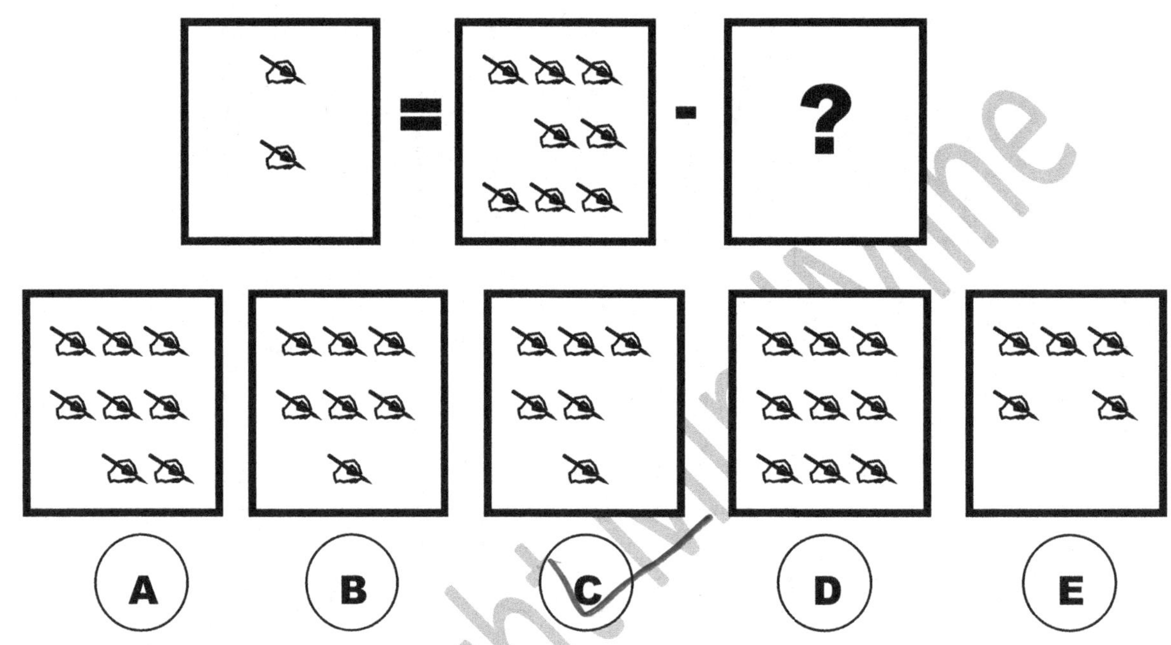

Question 10

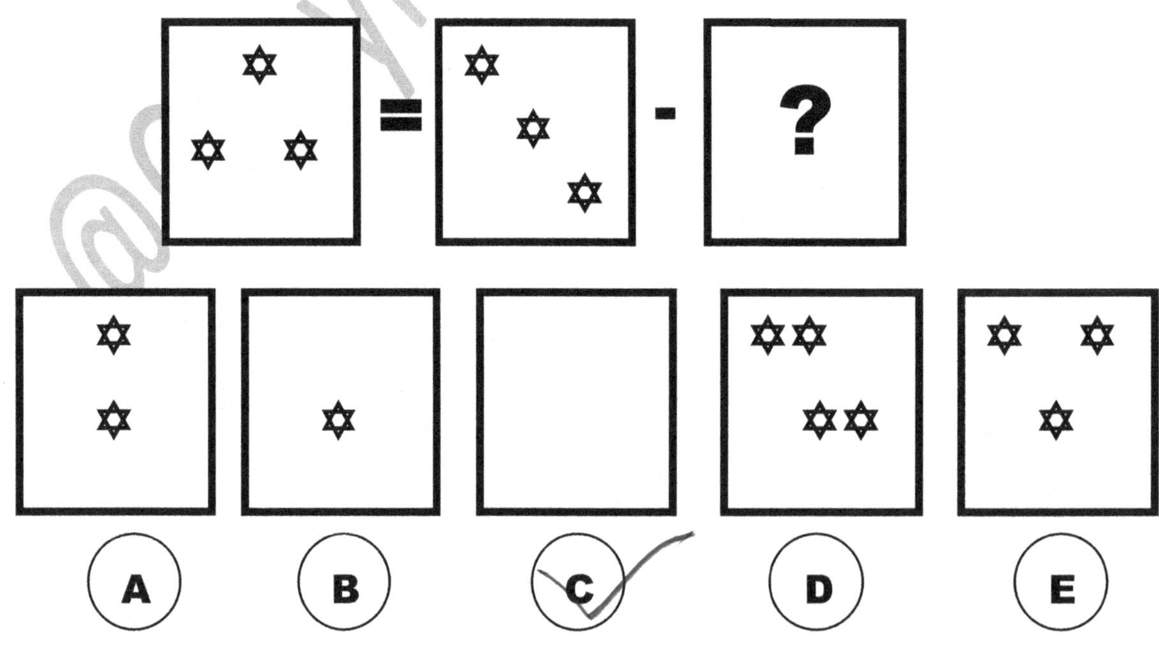

One-Step Equations

DIVISION

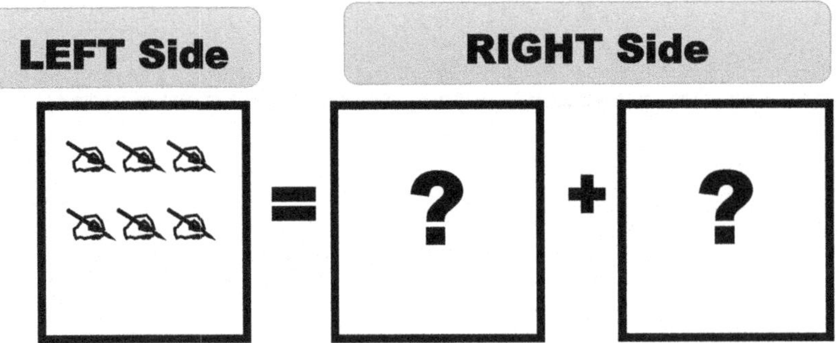

MATH WAY						
STEP#1	Count pictures on LEFT side	6	=	?	+	?
STEP#2	Solve DIVISION on RIGHT side	6	=	3	+	3
ANSWER				3		

It is good to know "ADDING DOUBLES" up to 10

1	+	1	=	2
2	+	2	=	4
3	+	3	=	6
4	+	4	=	8
5	+	5	=	10
6	+	6	=	12
7	+	7	=	14
8	+	8	=	16
9	+	9	=	18
10	+	10	=	20

Question 1

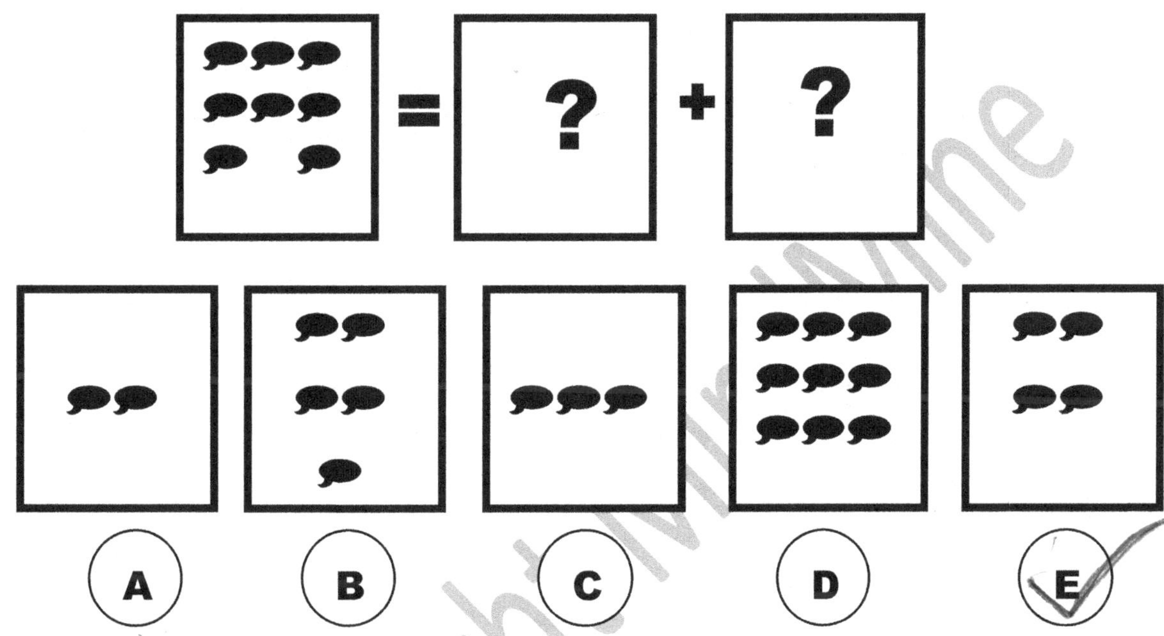

Question 2

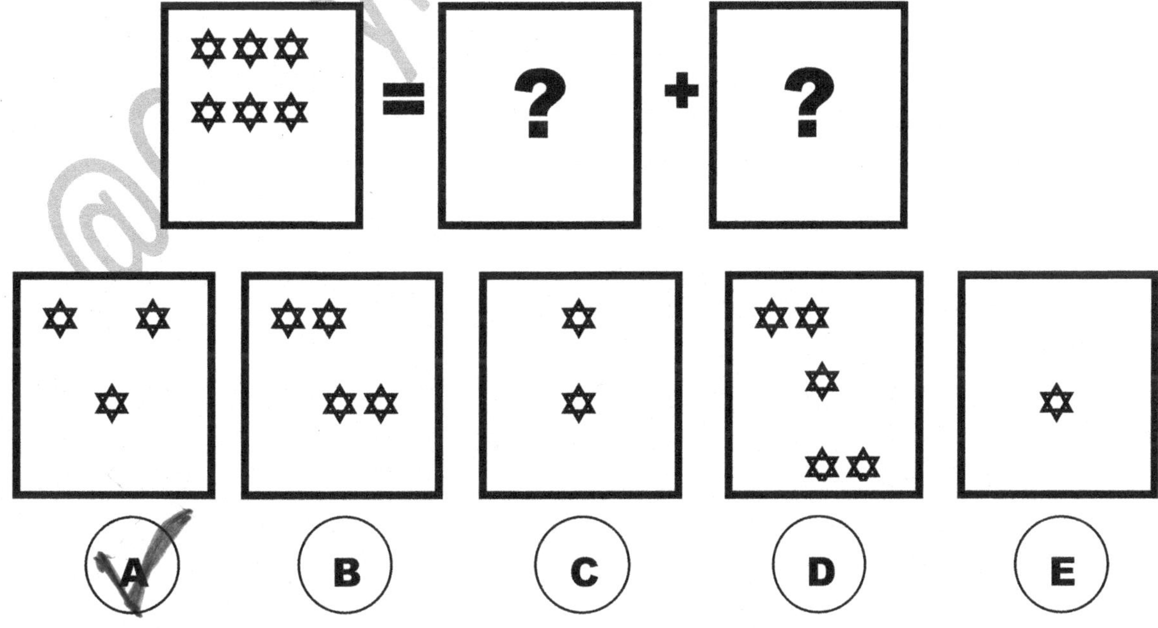

Question 3

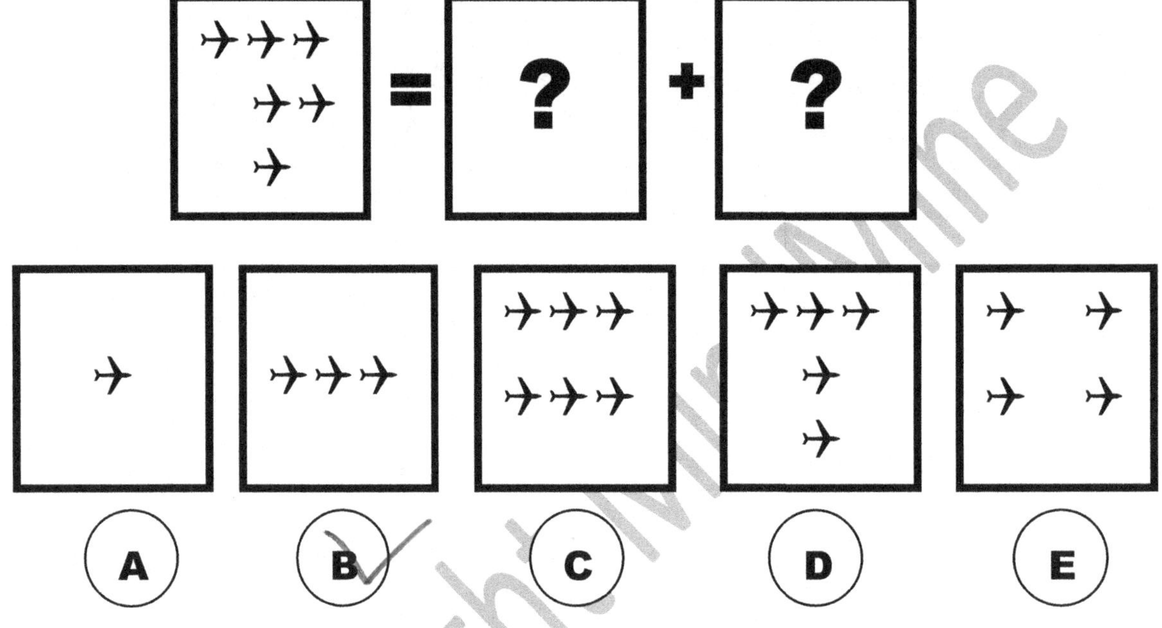

Question 4

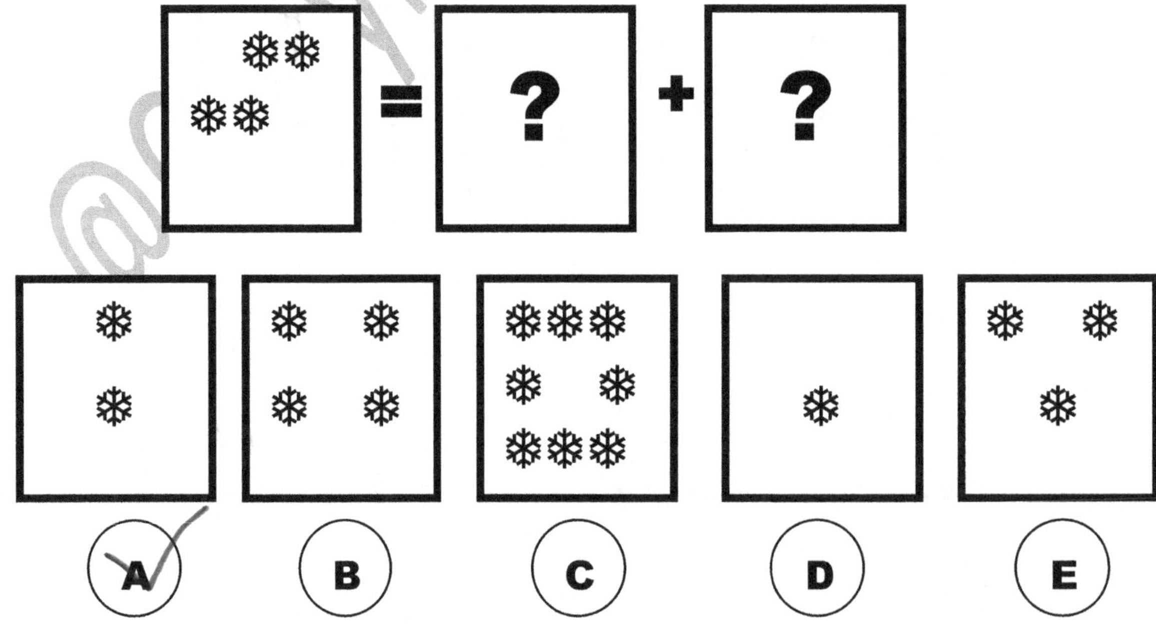

Question 5

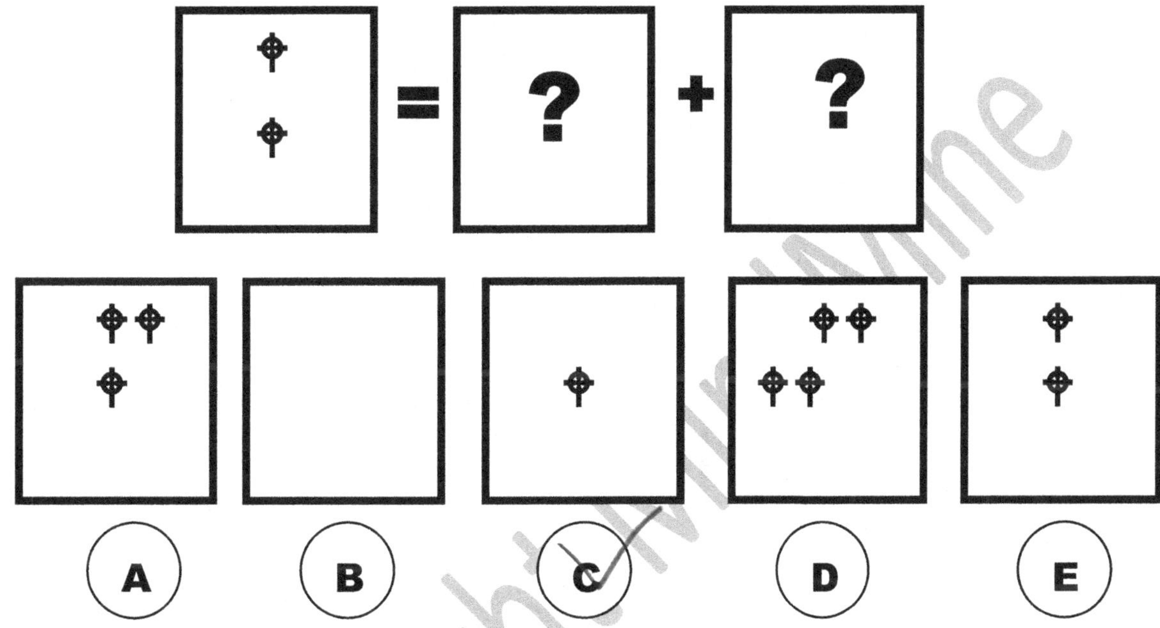

Question 6

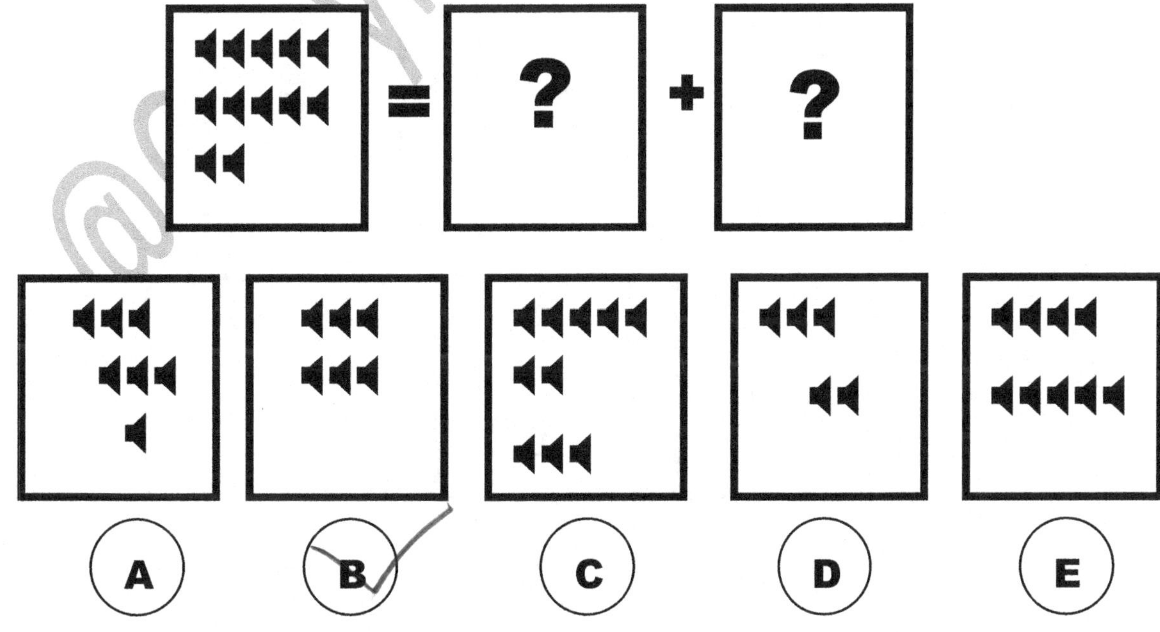

Question 7

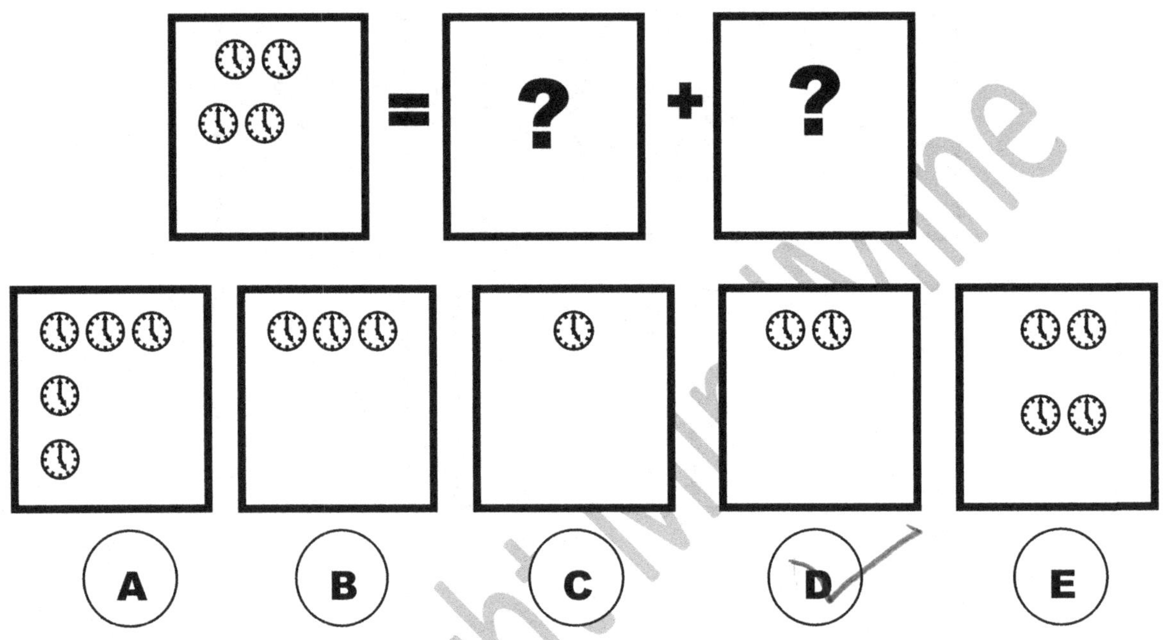

Question 8

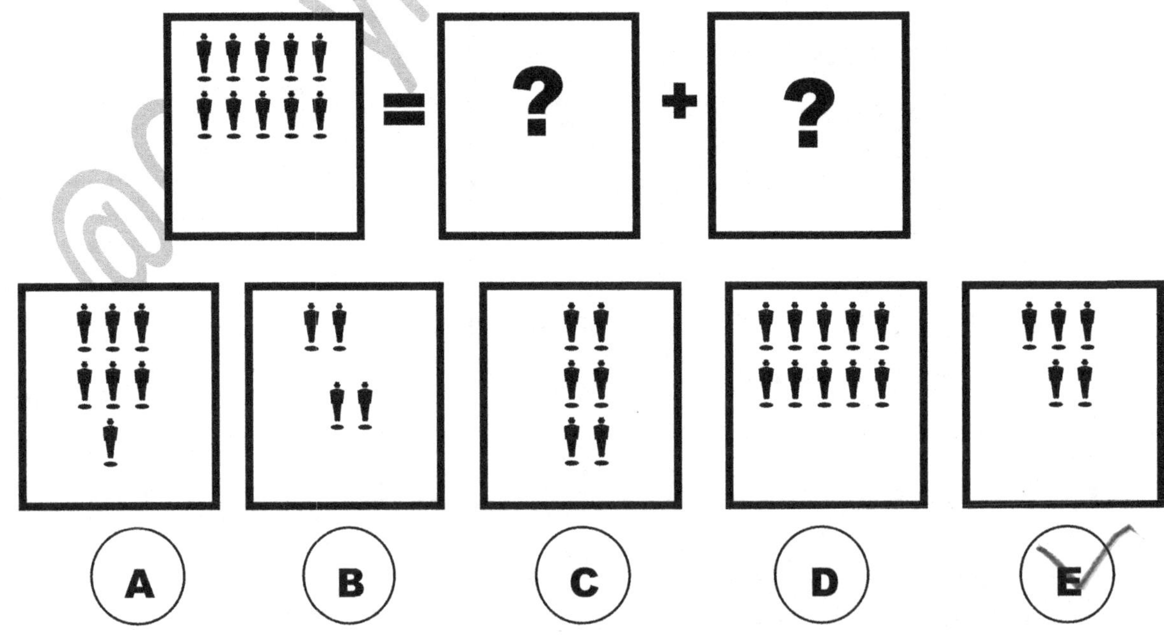

Question 9

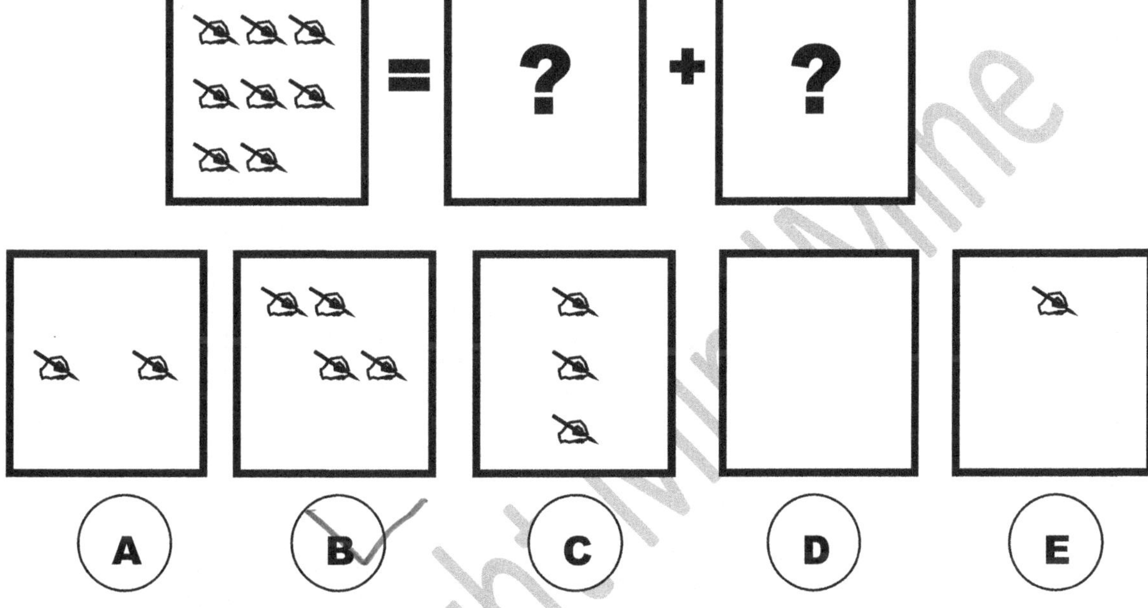

Question 10

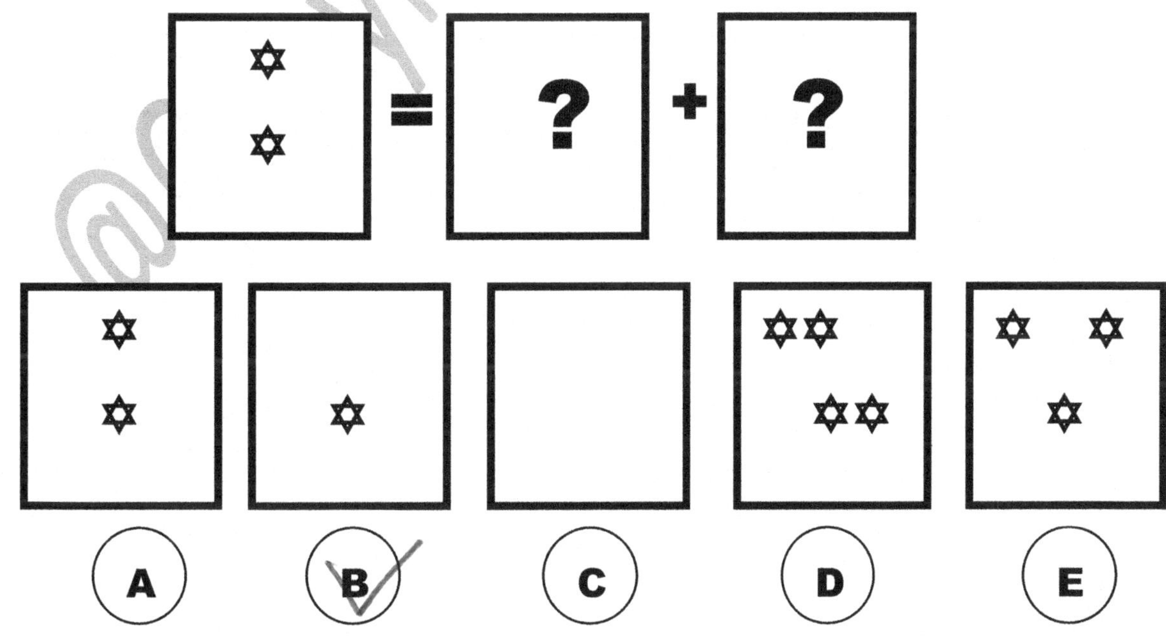

Two-Step Equations

Addition & Addition

LEFT Side **RIGHT Side**

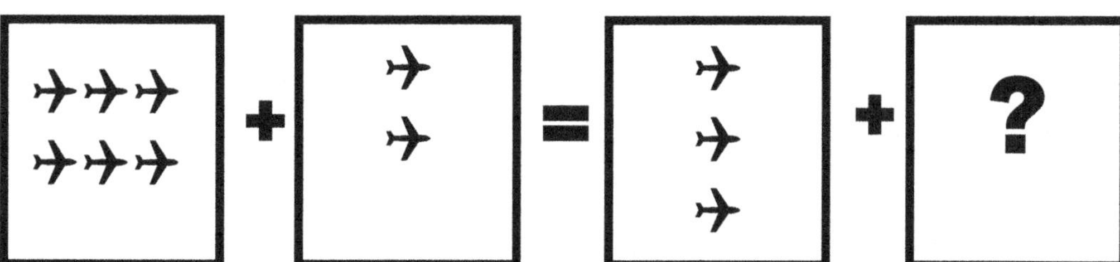

MATH WAY								
STEP#1	Count pictures on BOTH sides	6	+	2	=	3	+	?
STEP#2	Solve ADDITION on LEFT side	8			=	3	+	**?**
STEP#3	Solve ADDITION on RIGHT side	8			=	3	+	**5**
ANSWER					**5**			

LEFT Side **RIGHT Side**

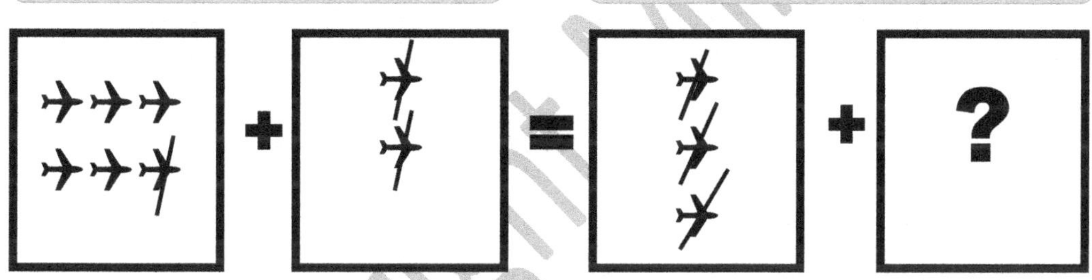

COUNTING TECHNIQUE						
STEP#1	-Count pictures on RIGHT side. -Strike out as you count	3				?
STEP#2	-Strike out same number of pictures on LEFT side.			3		
STEP#3	Count REMAINING pictures on LEFT side	5				
ANSWER						5

Question 1

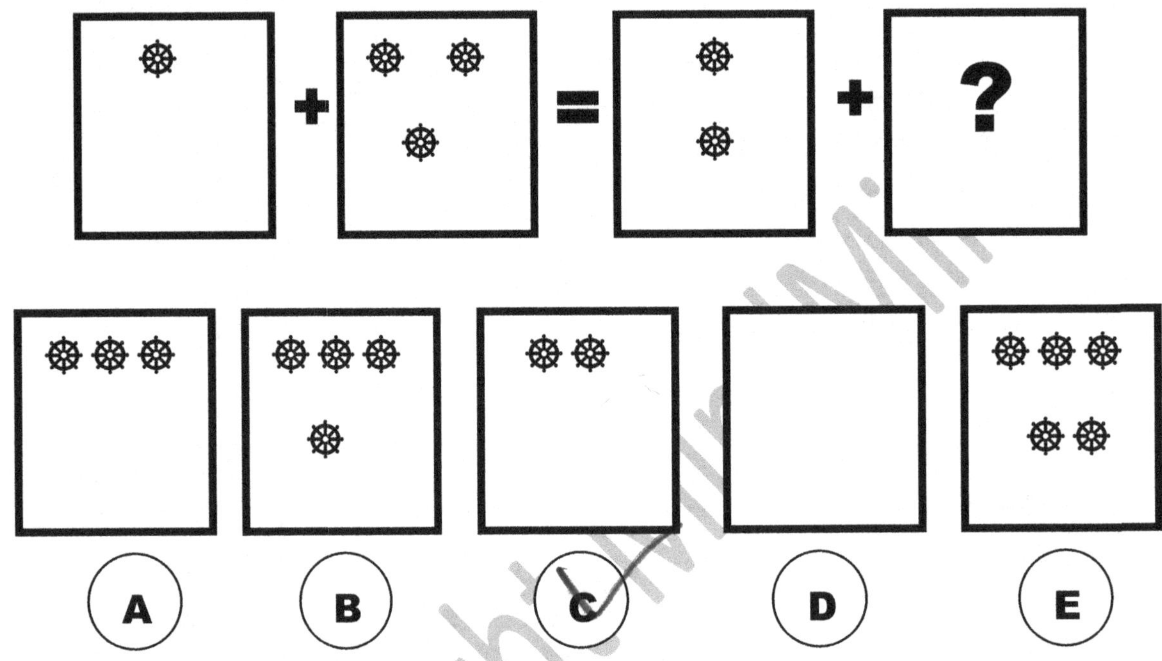

Question 2

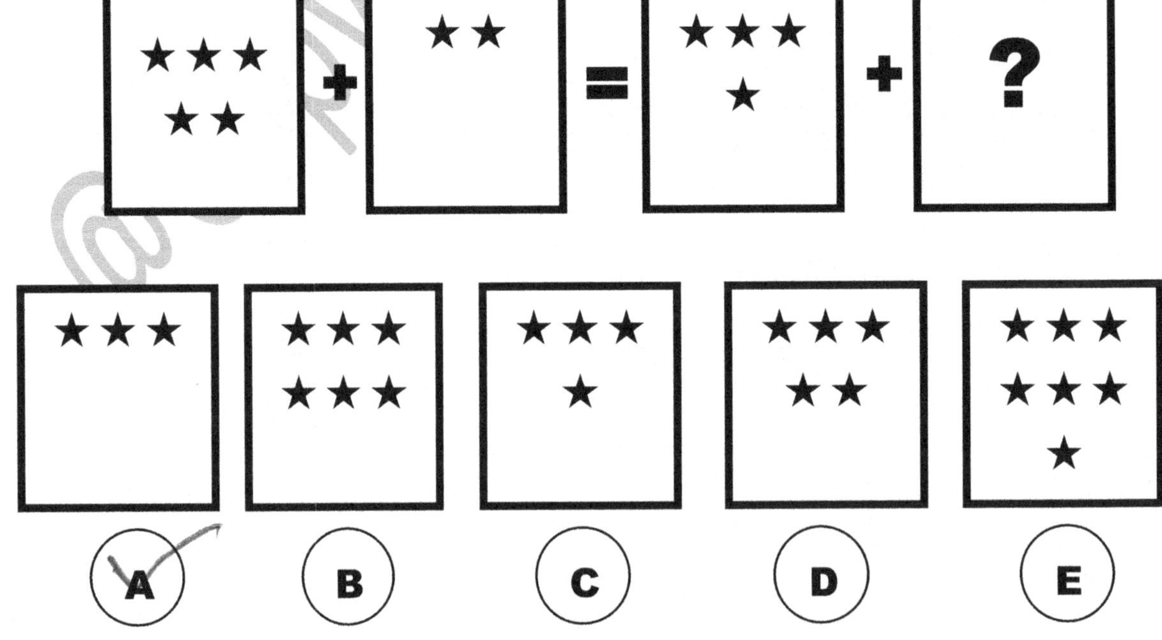

Question 3

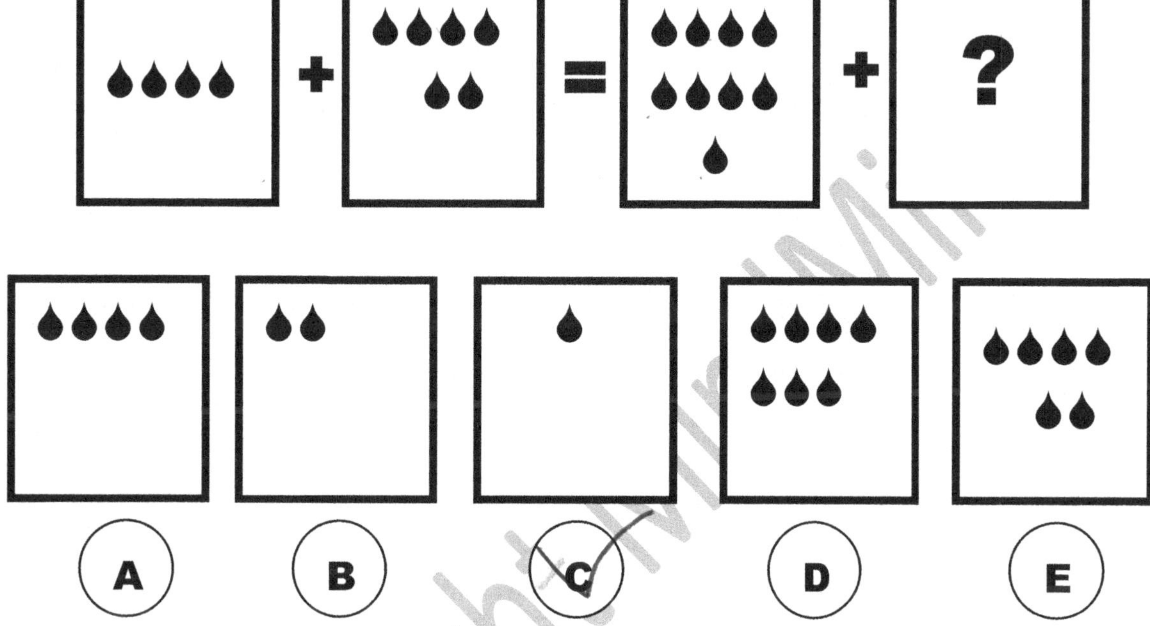

Question 4

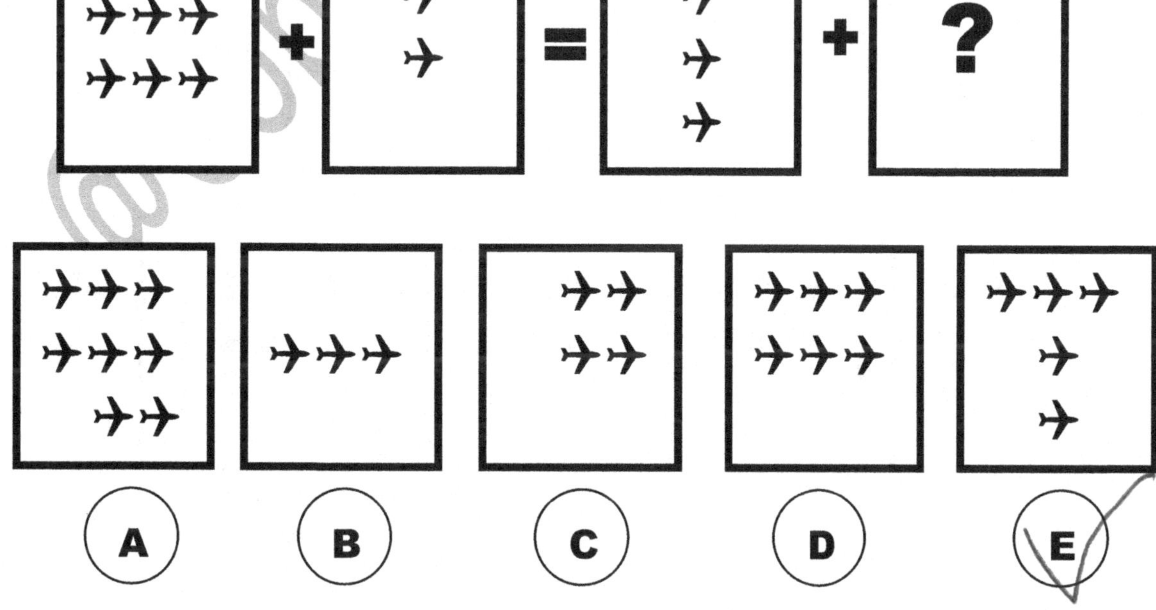

Question 5

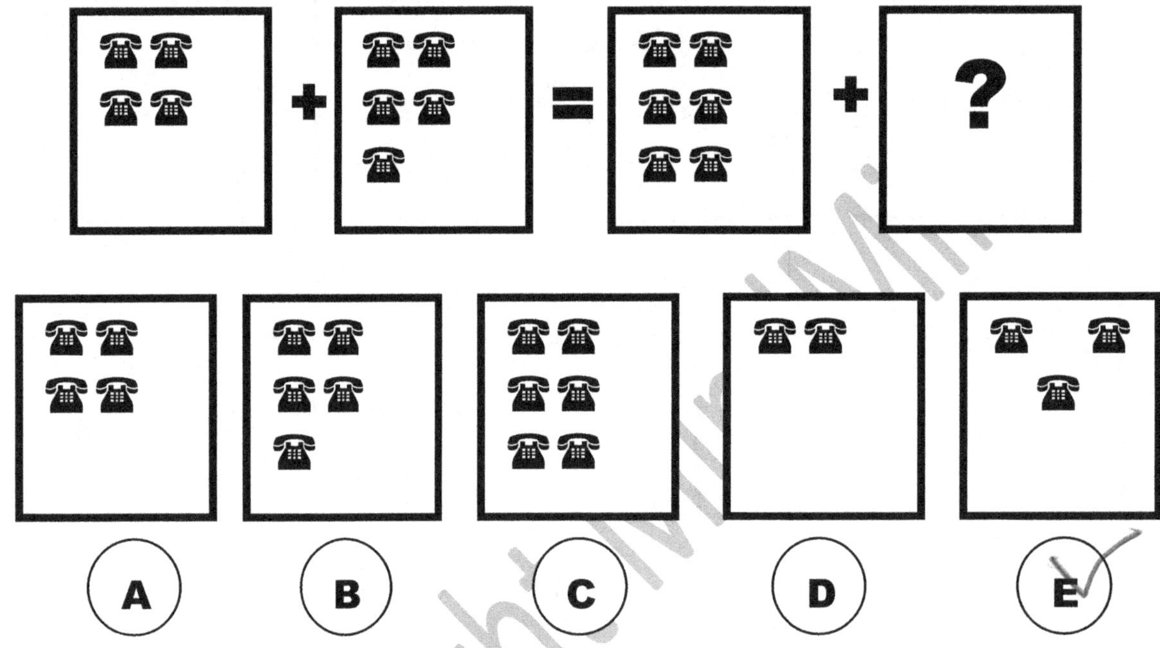

Question 6

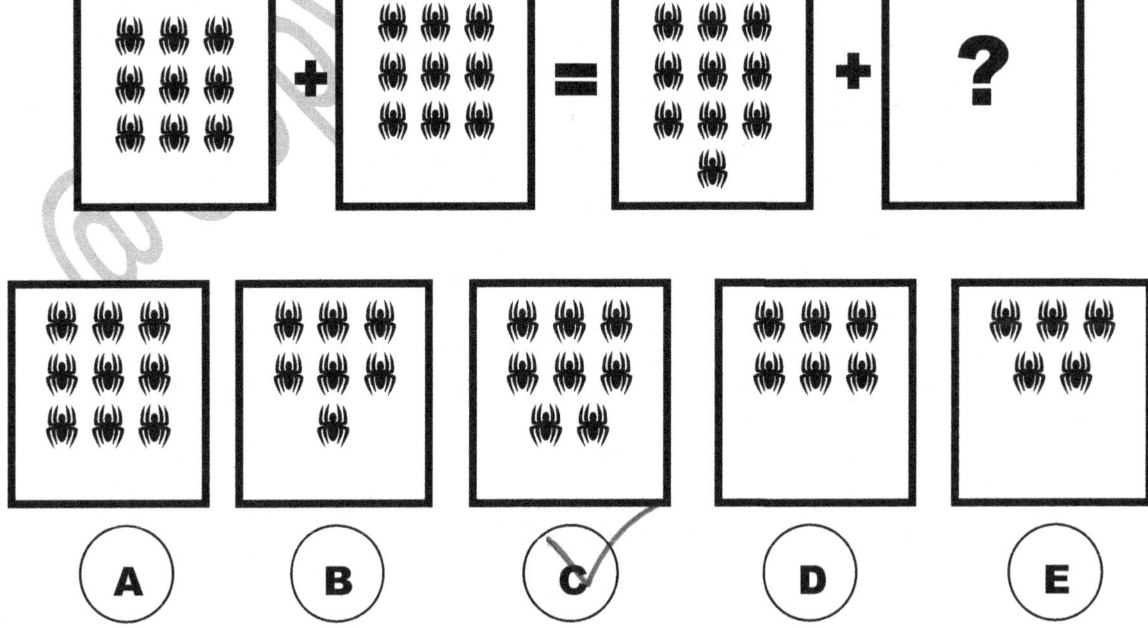

Question 7

?

A B C D E

Question 8

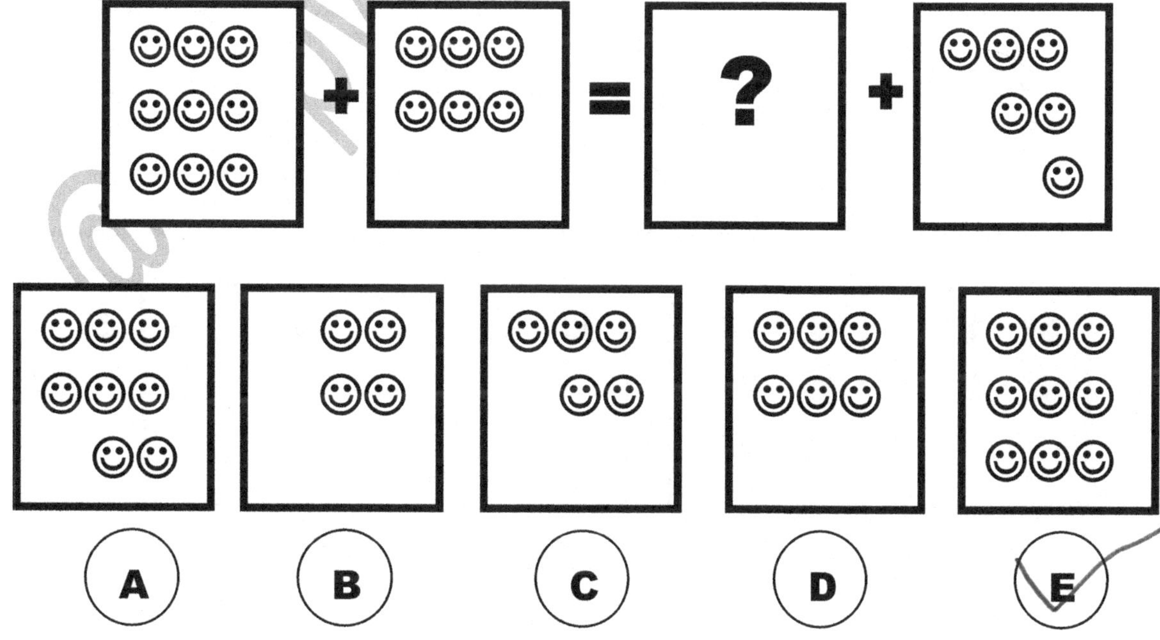

Question 9

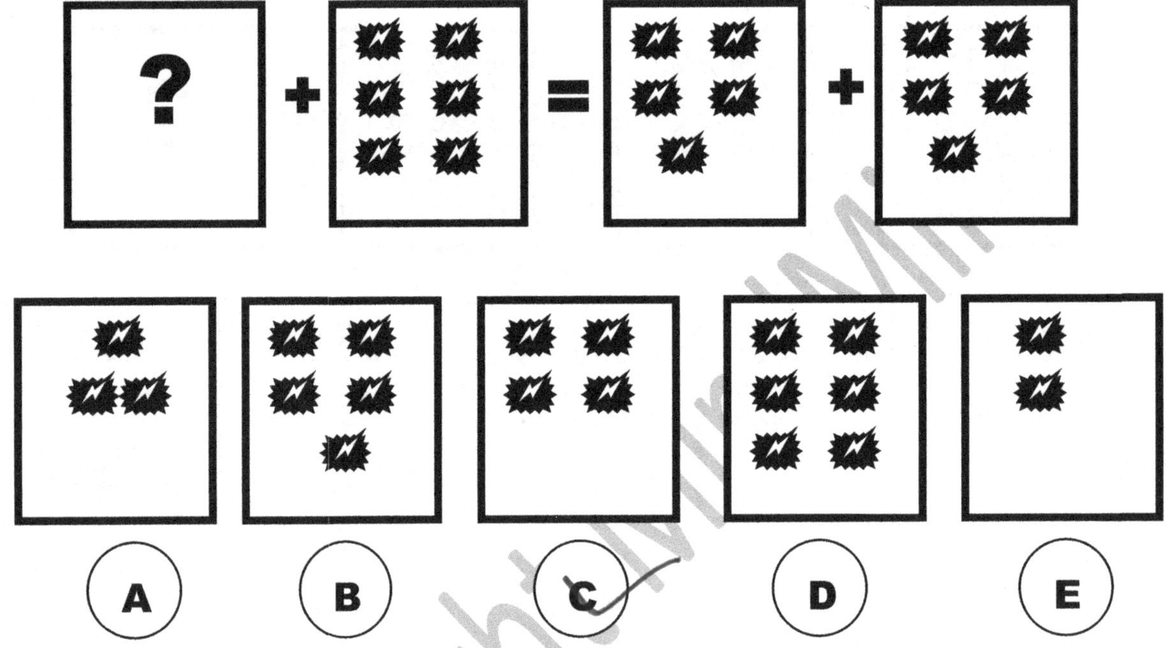

Question 10

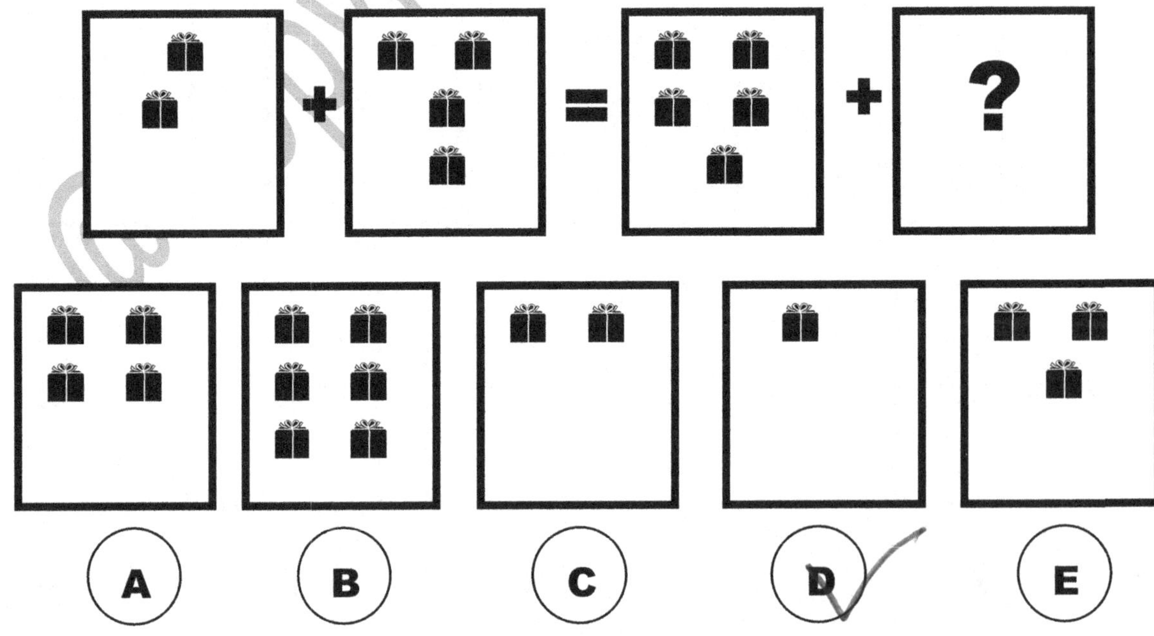

Two-Step Equations

Addition & Subtraction

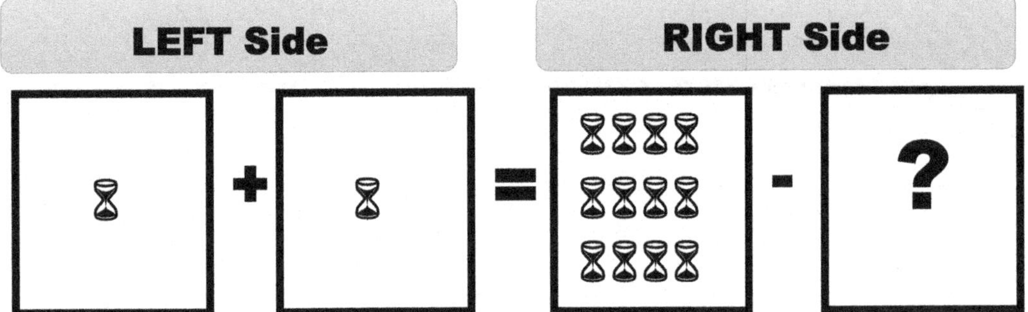

MATH WAY								
STEP#1	Count pictures on BOTH sides	1	+	1	=	12	-	?
STEP#2	Solve ADDITION on LEFT side	2			=	12	-	?
STEP#3	Solve SUBTRACTION on RIGHT side	2			=	12	-	**10**
ANSWER				**10**				

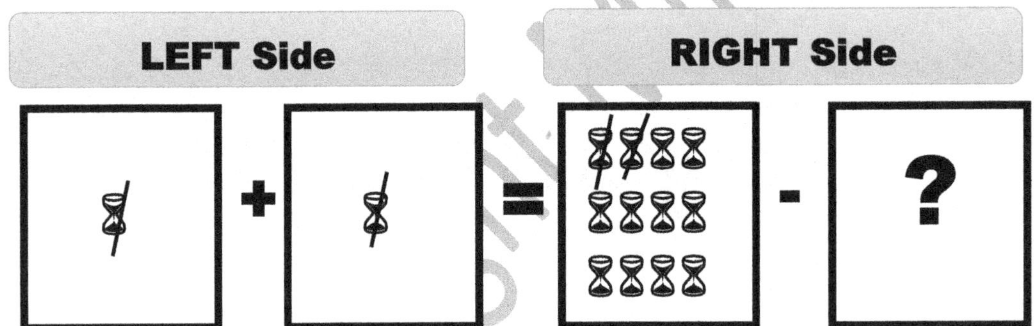

COUNTING TECHNIQUE						
STEP#1	-Count pictures on LEFT side. -Strike out as you count	2				?
STEP#2	-Strike out same number of pictures on RIGHT side.			2		
STEP#3	Count REMAINING pictures on RIGHT side	10				
ANSWER						10

Question 1

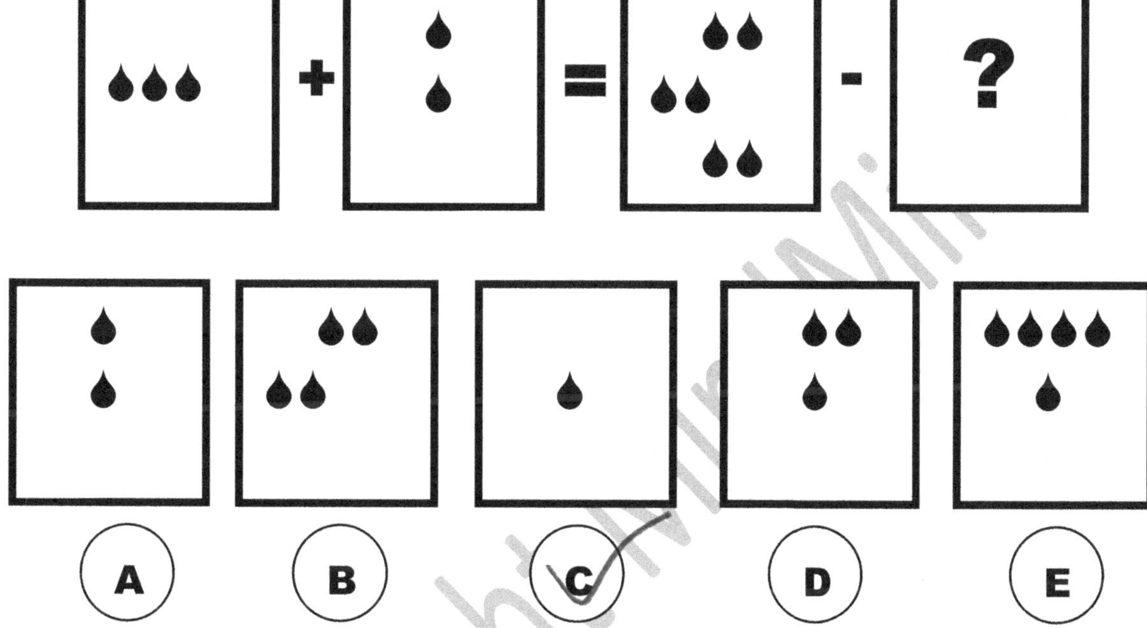

Question 2

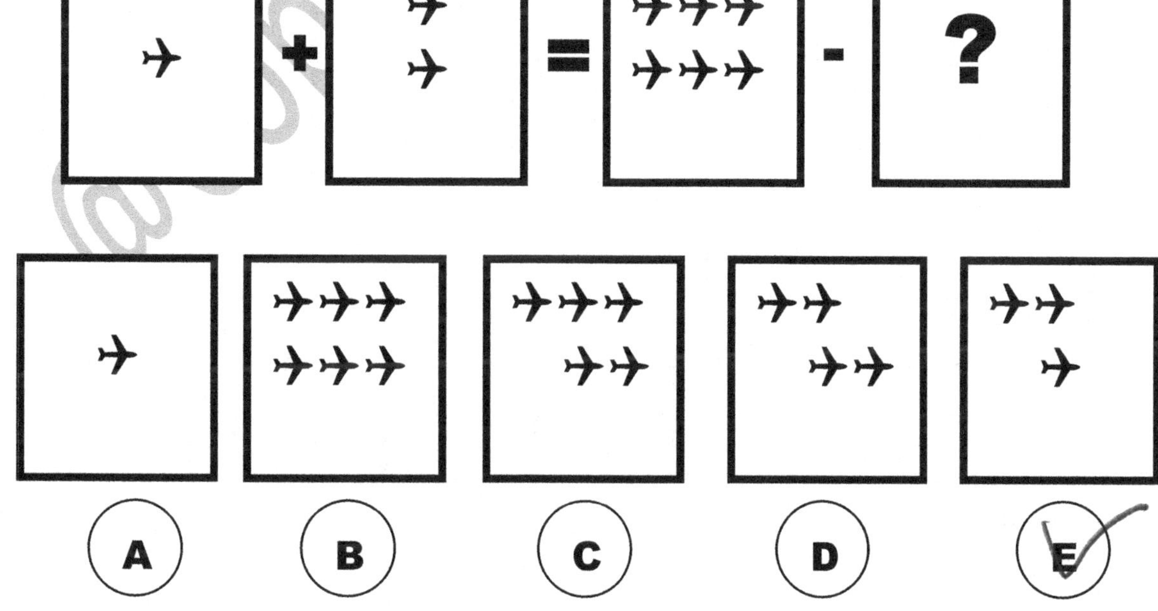

Question 3

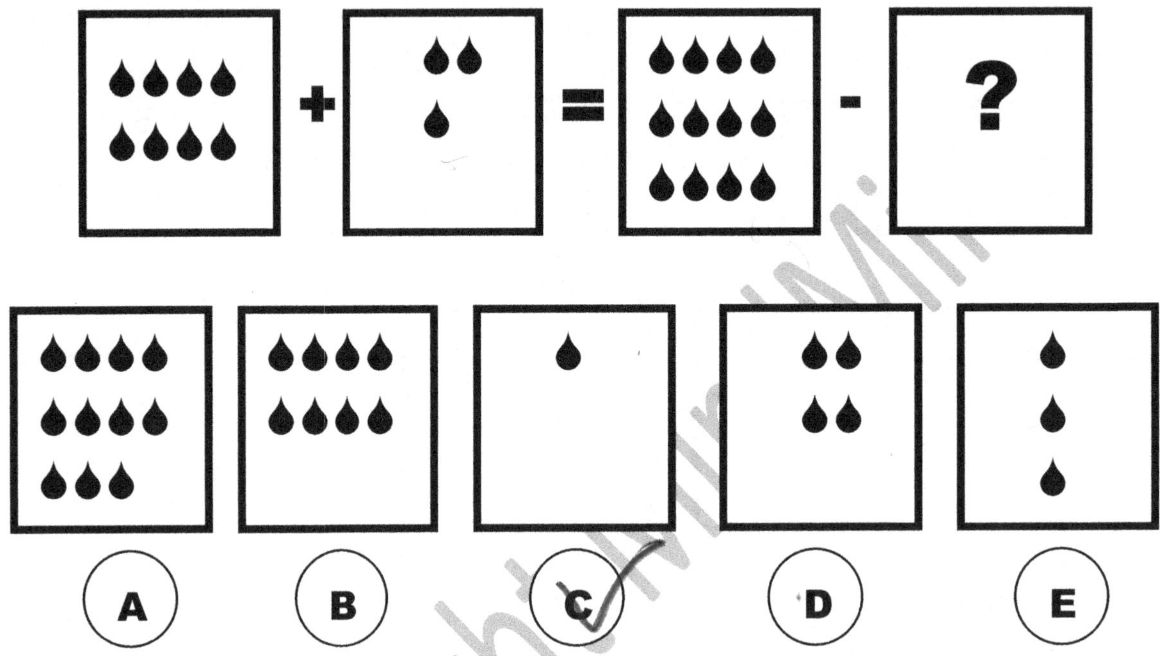

Question 4

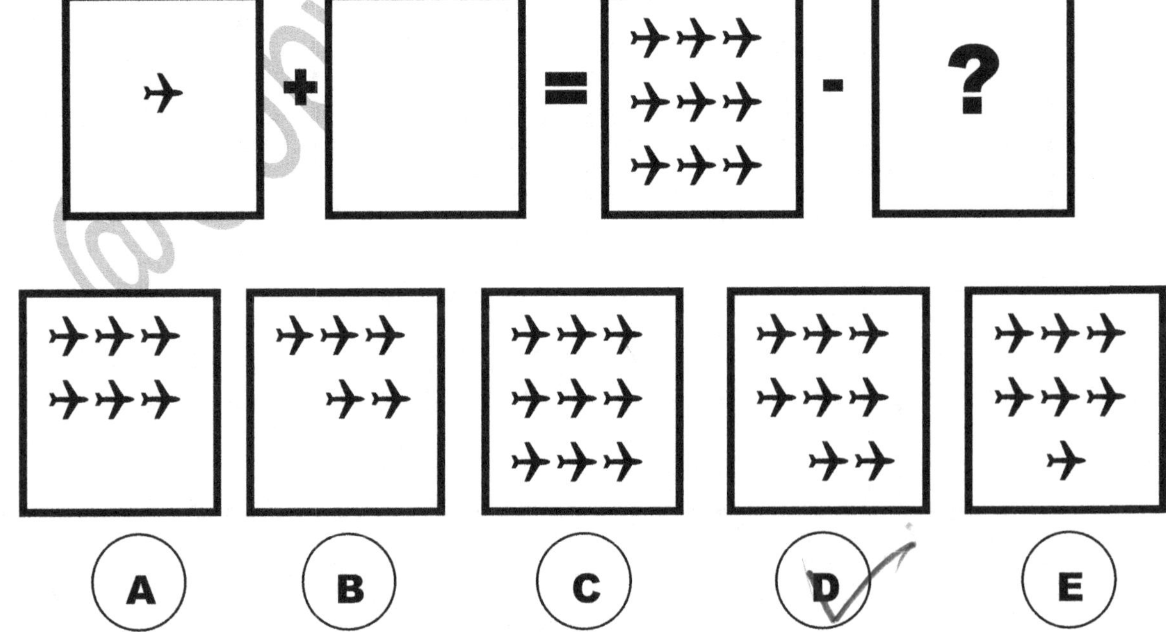

Question 5

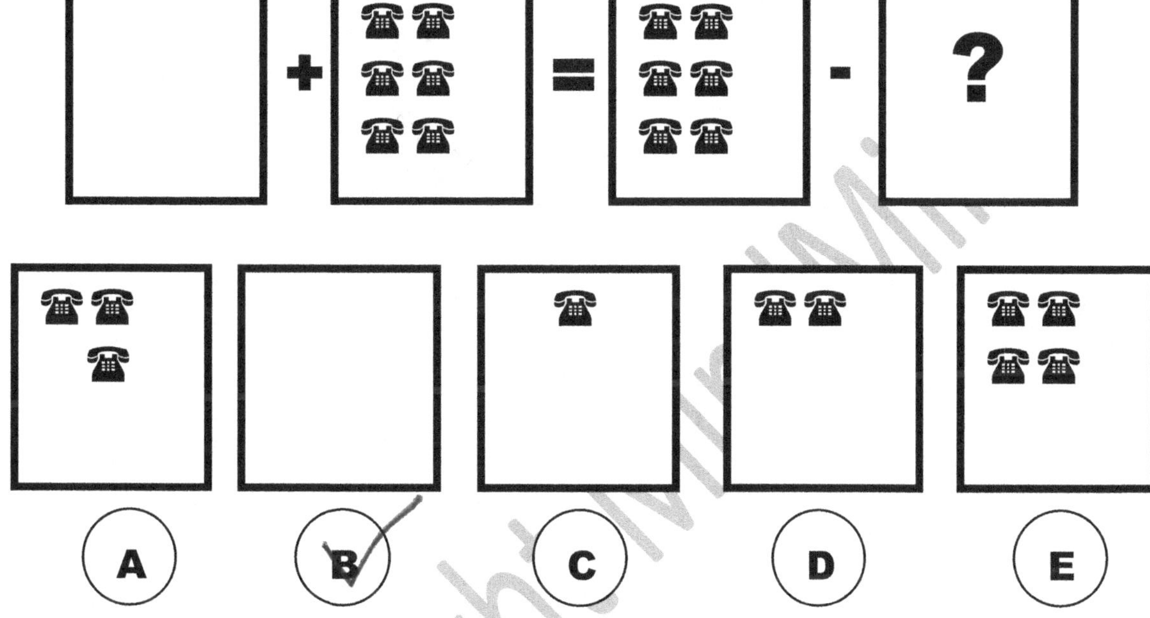

Question 6

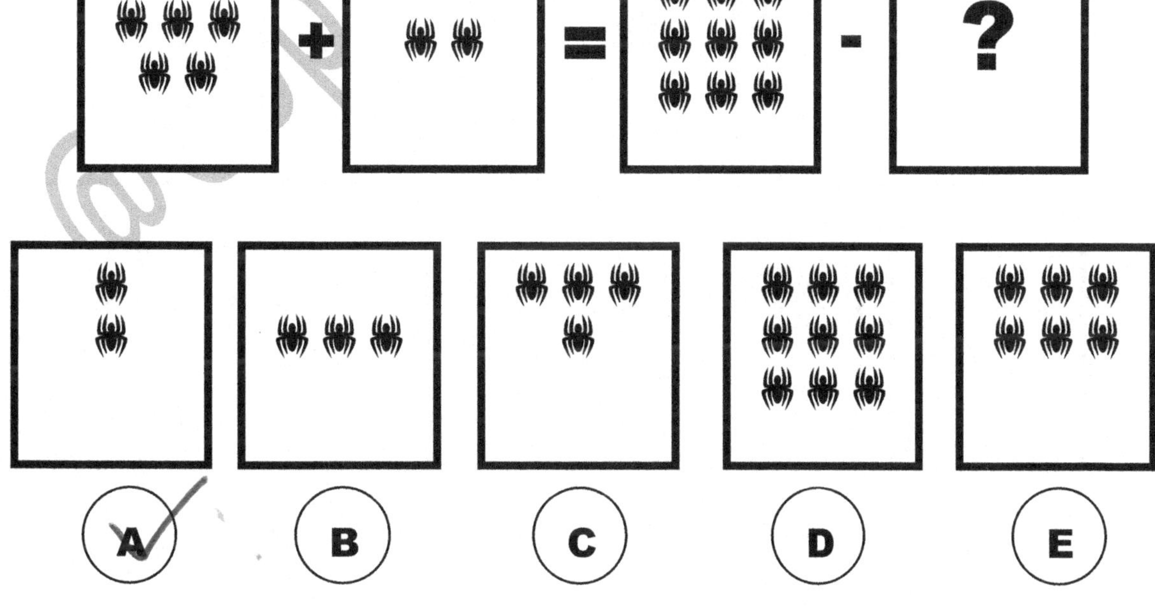

Question 7

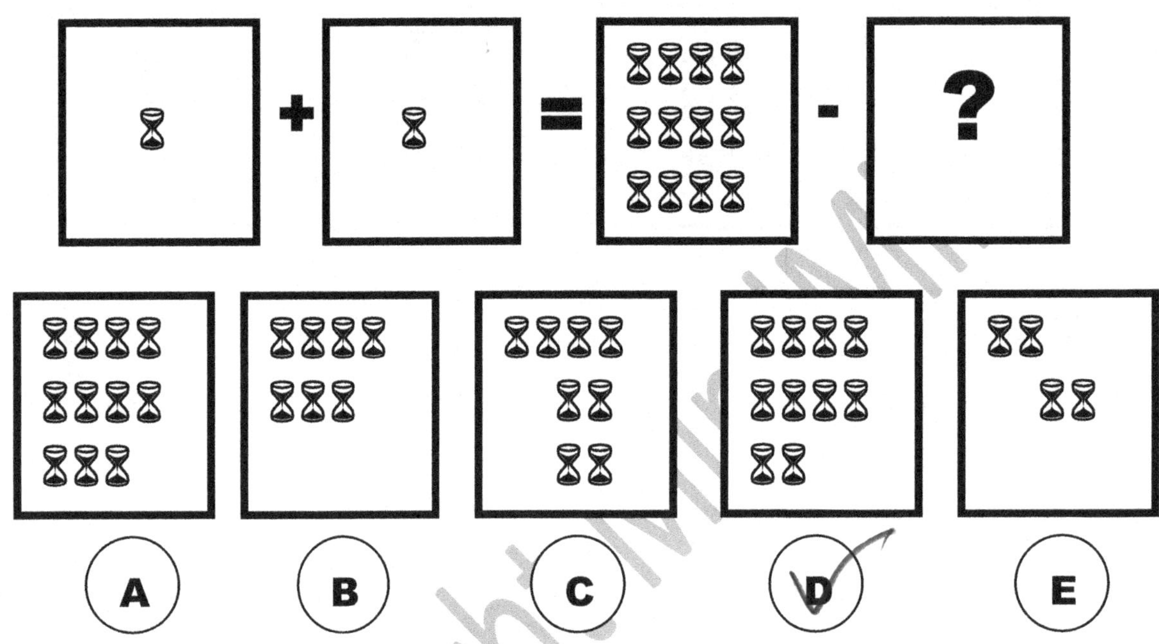

Question 8

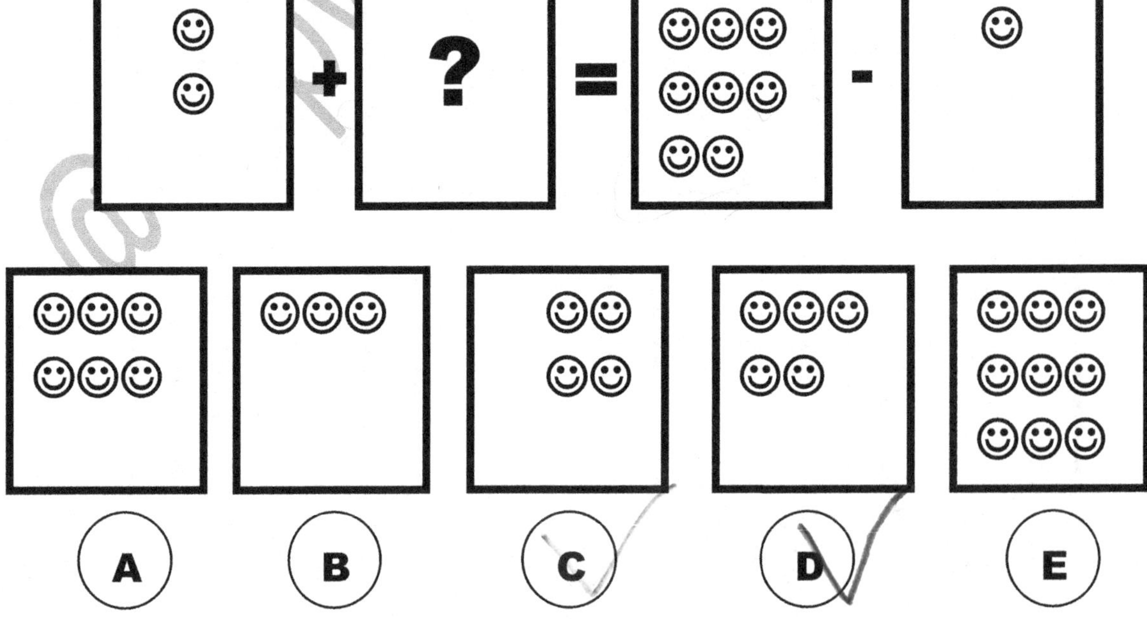

Question 9

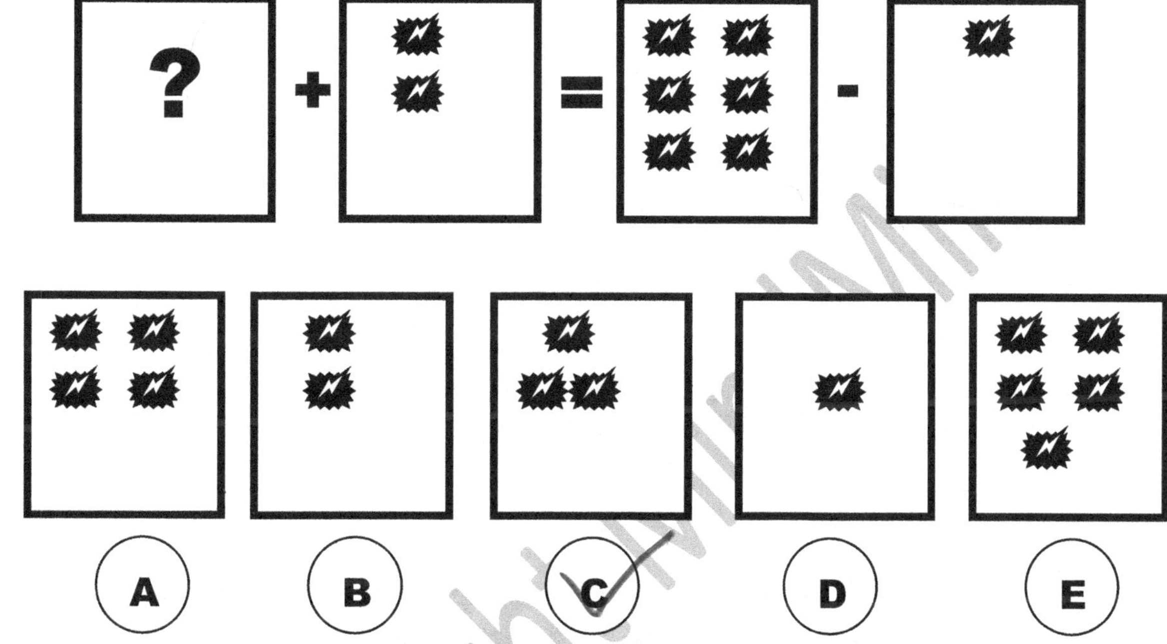

Question 10

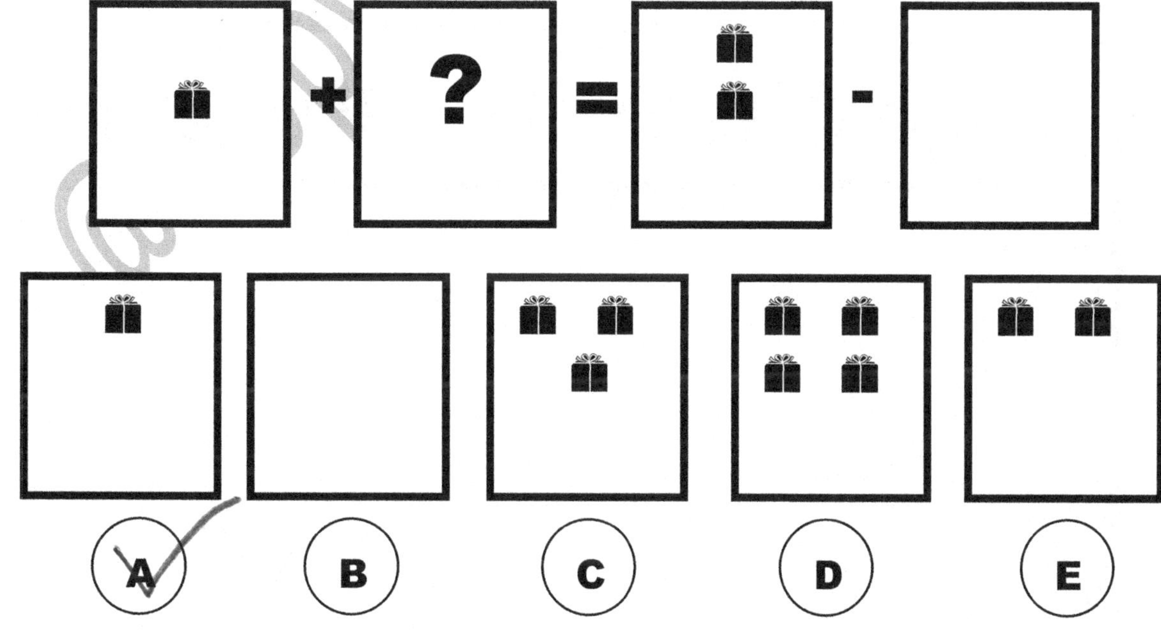

Two-Step Equations

Addition & Division

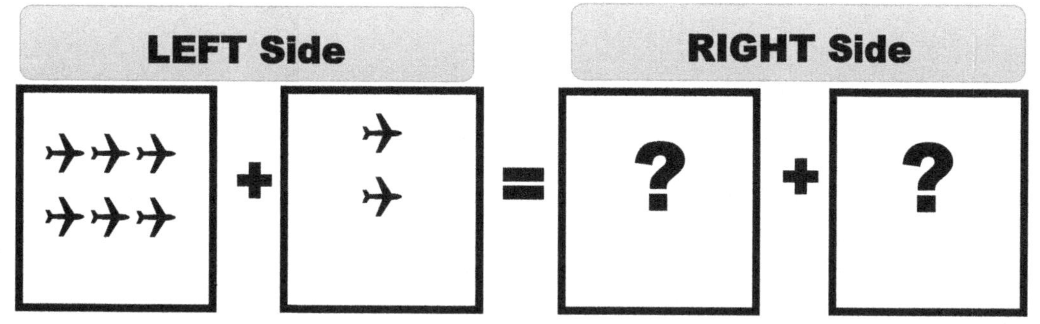

MATH WAY						
STEP#1	Count pictures on LEFT side	8	=	?	+	?
STEP#2	Solve DIVISION on RIGHT side	8	=	4	+	**4**
ANSWER					**4**	

It is good to know "ADDING DOUBLES" up to 10

1	+	1	=	2
2	+	2	=	4
3	+	3	=	6
4	+	4	=	8
5	+	5	=	10
6	+	6	=	12
7	+	7	=	14
8	+	8	=	16
9	+	9	=	18
10	+	10	=	20

Question 1

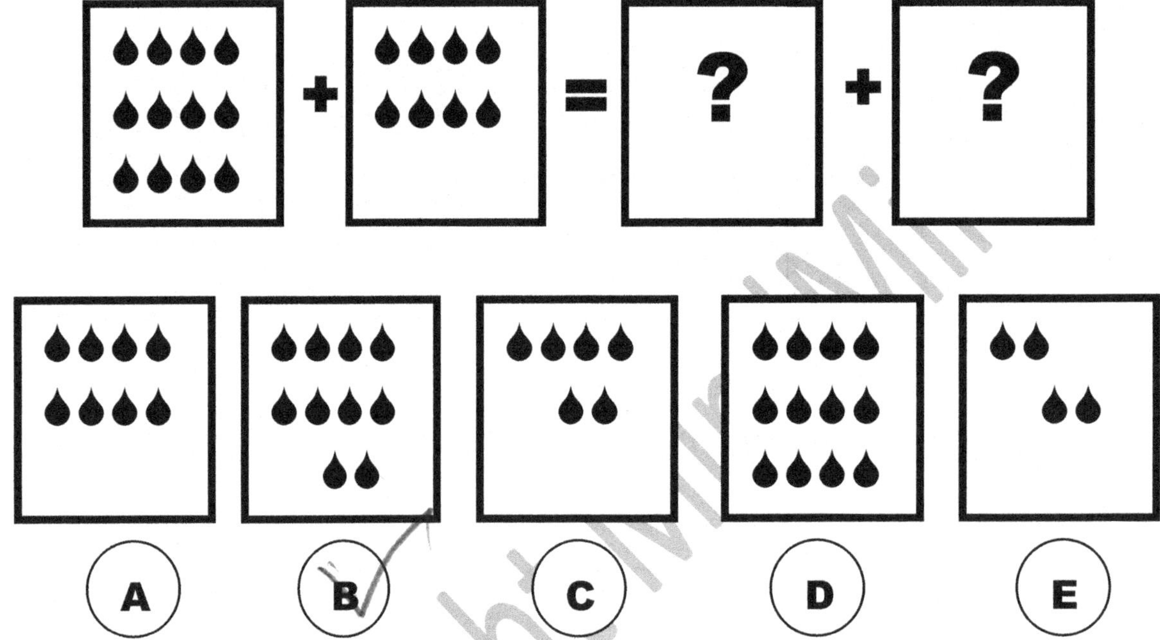

Question 2

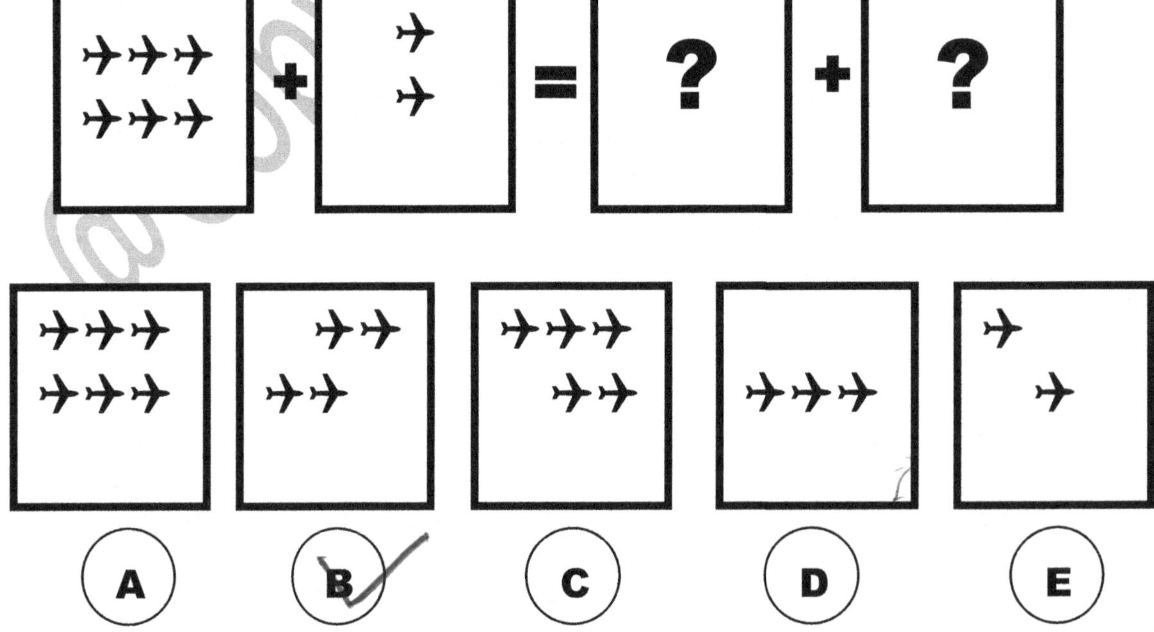

Question 3

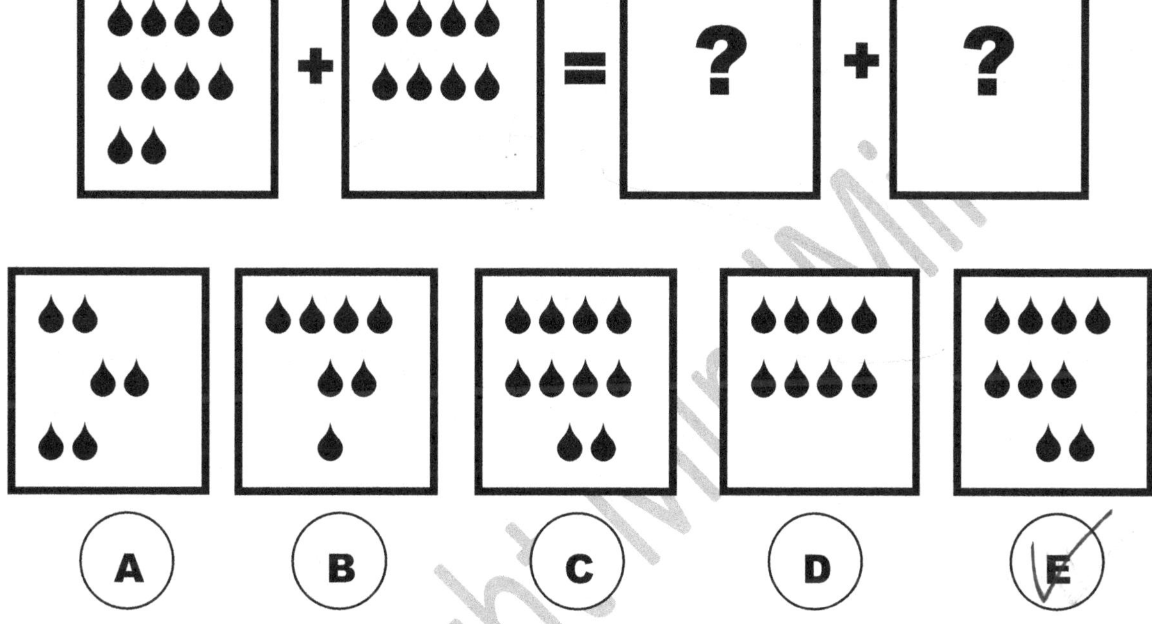

Question 4

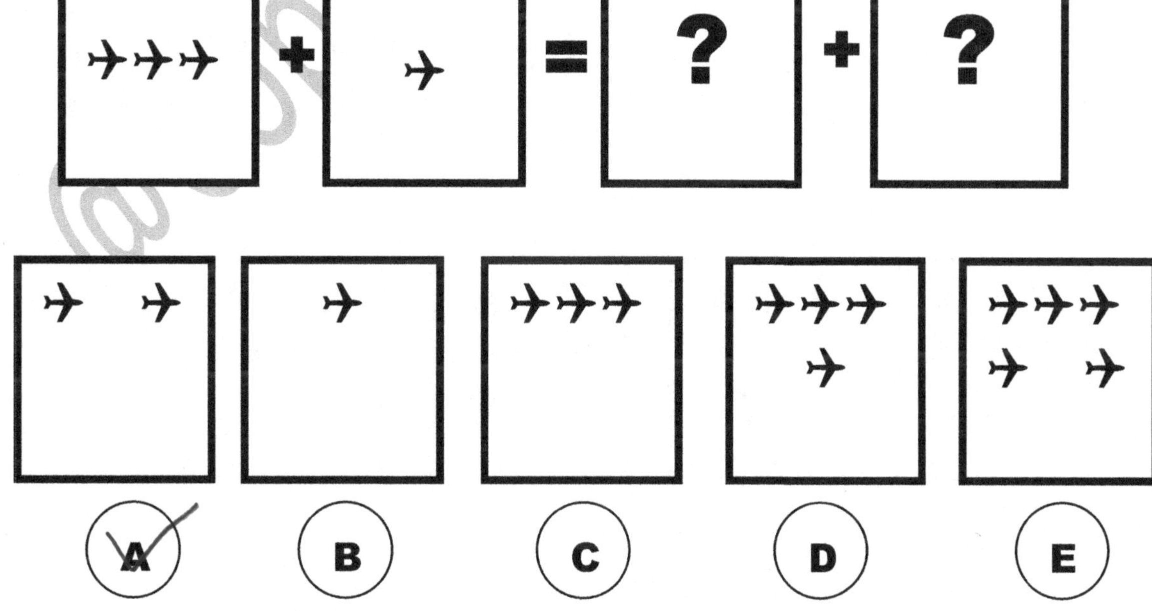

Question 5

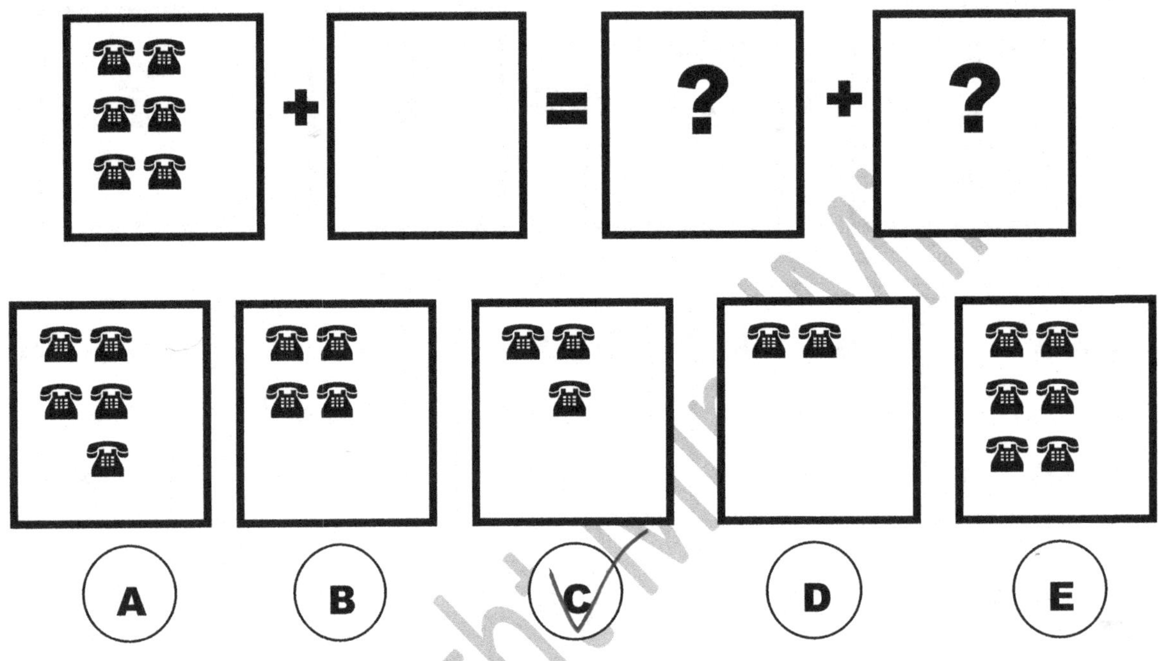

Question 6

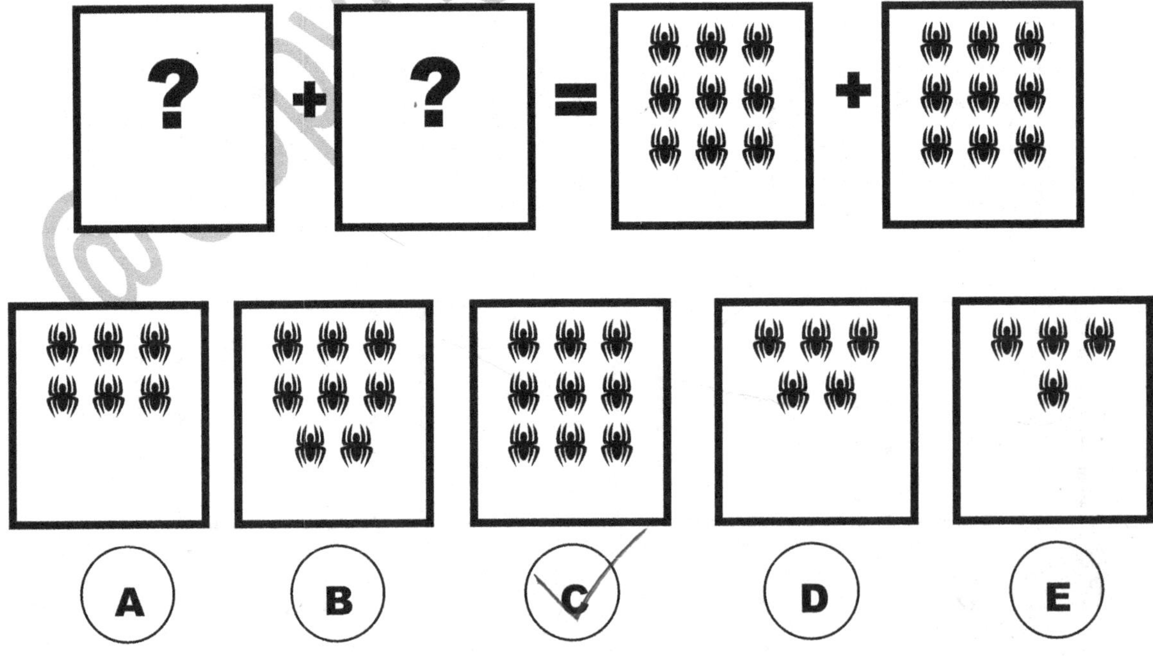

Question 7

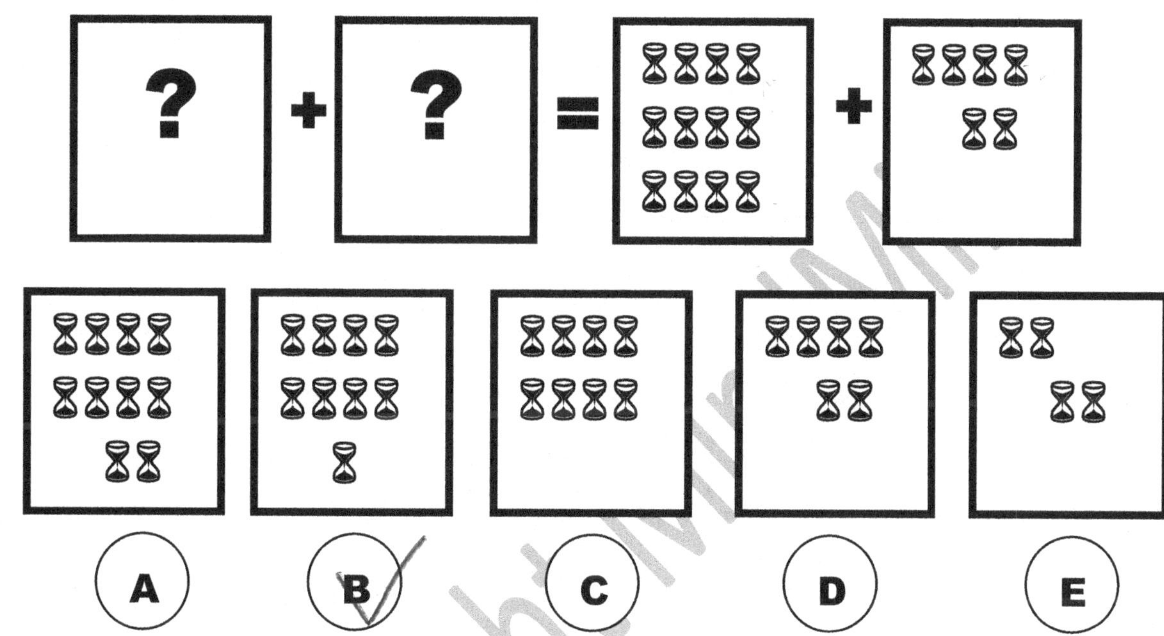

Question 8

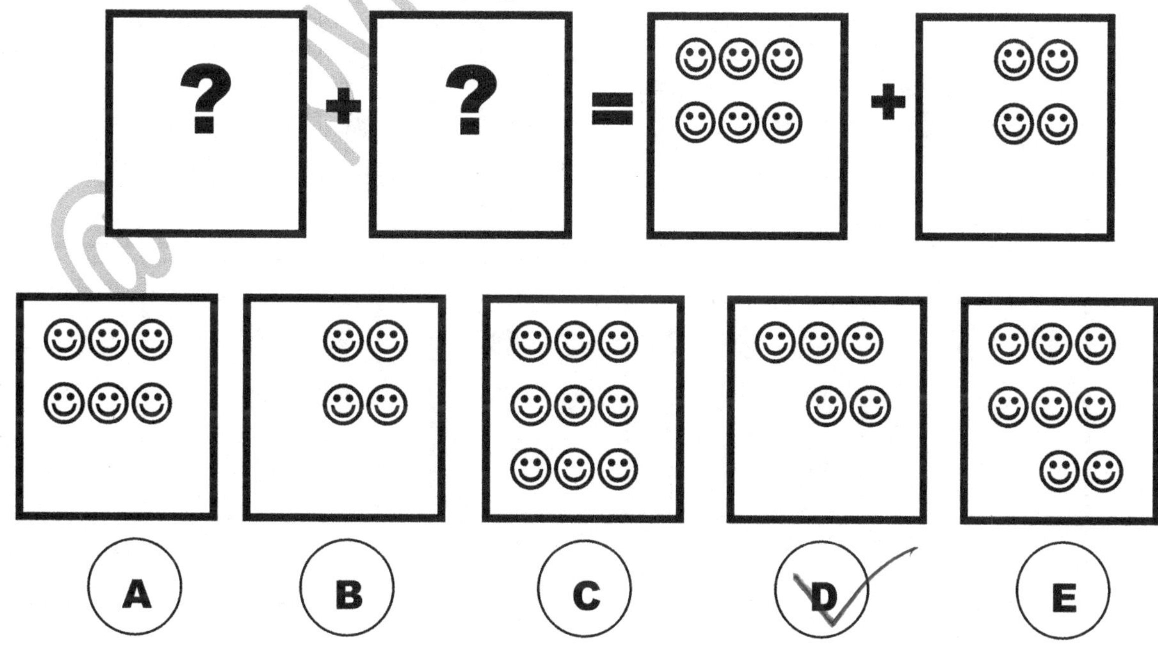

Question 9

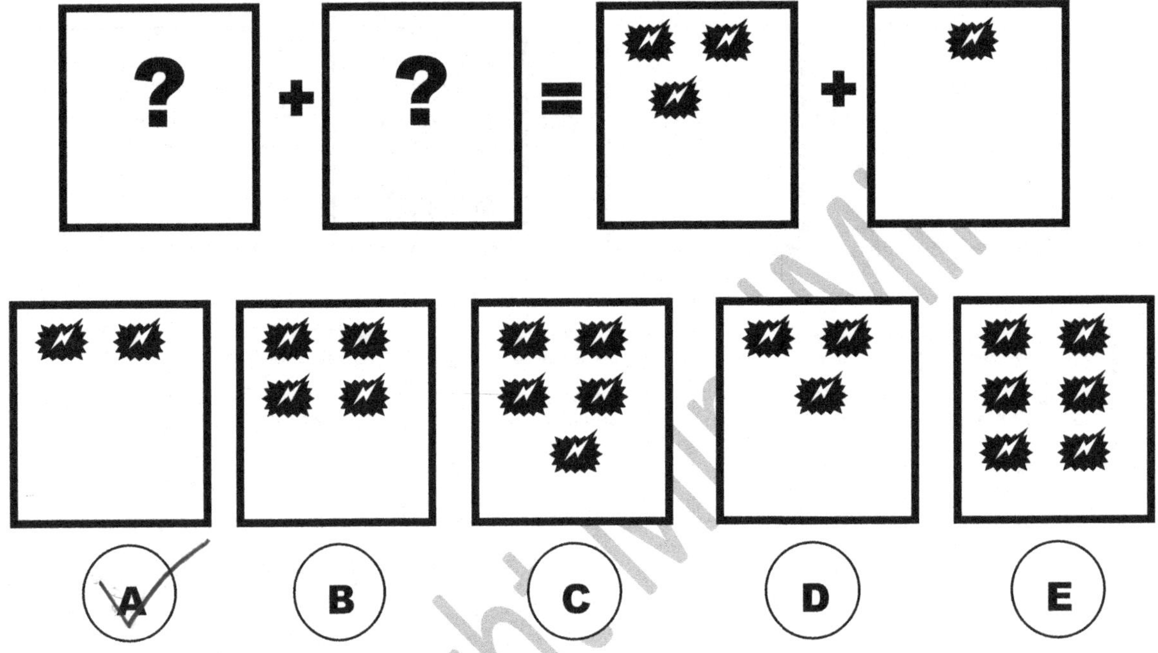

Question 10

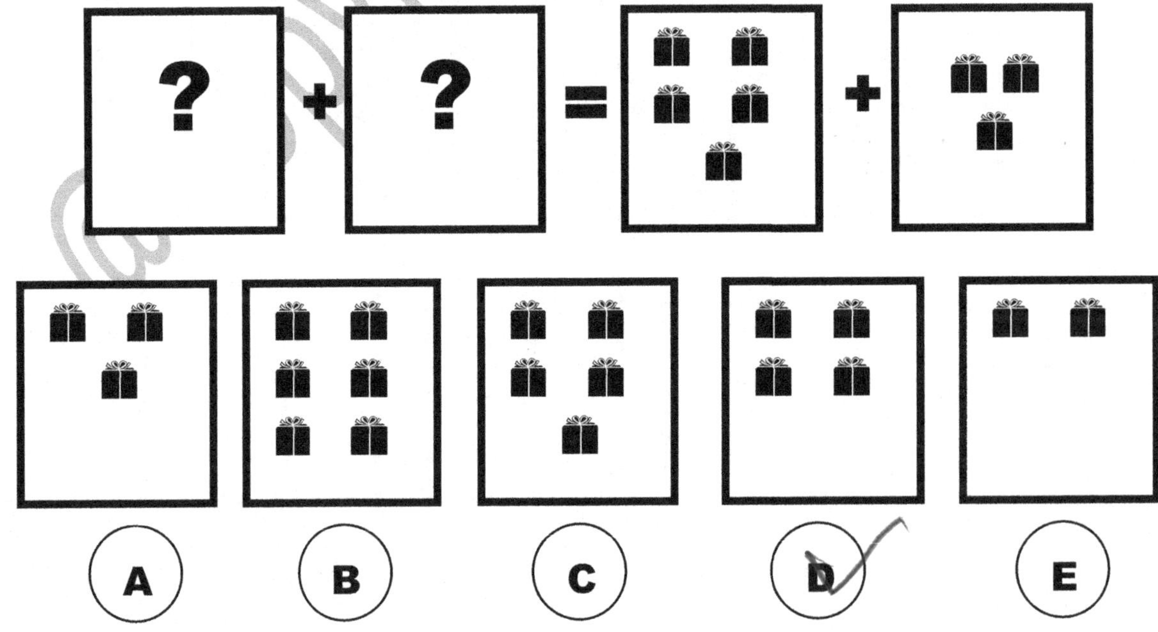

Multi-Step Equations Using

Addition

Subtraction

&

Division

LEFT Side		RIGHT Side		

 + 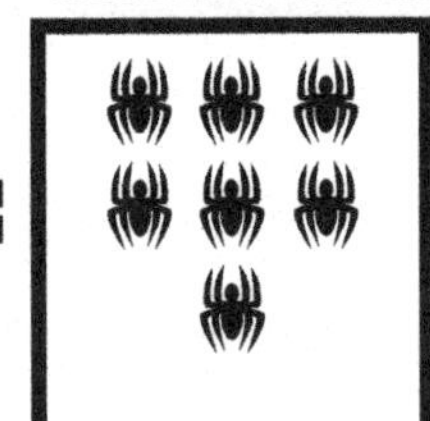 + ? + 

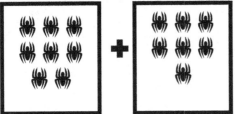

MATH WAY										
STEP#1	Count pictures on BOTH sides	8	+	7	=	7	+	?	+	3
STEP#2	Solve ADDITION on LEFT side	15			=	7	+	?	+	3
STEP#3	Solve ADDITION on RIGHT side	15			=	10	+	?		
STEP#4	Solve Addition on RIGHT side	15			=	10	+	**5**		
ANSWER					**5**					

LEFT Side

RIGHT Side

 + 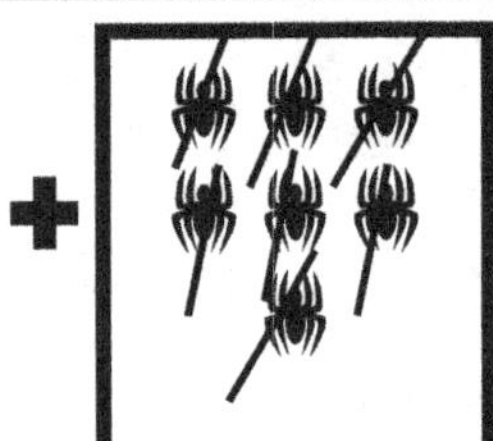 =  +  ? + 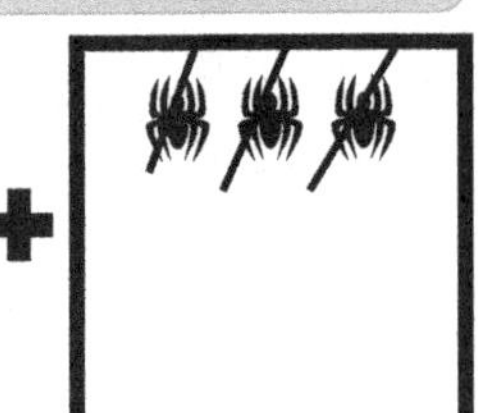

COUNTING TECHNIQUE				
STEP#1	-Count pictures on RIGHT side. -Strike out as you count		10	?
STEP#2	-Strike out same number of pictures on LEFT side.	10		
STEP#3	Count REMAINING pictures on LEFT side	5		
ANSWER				5

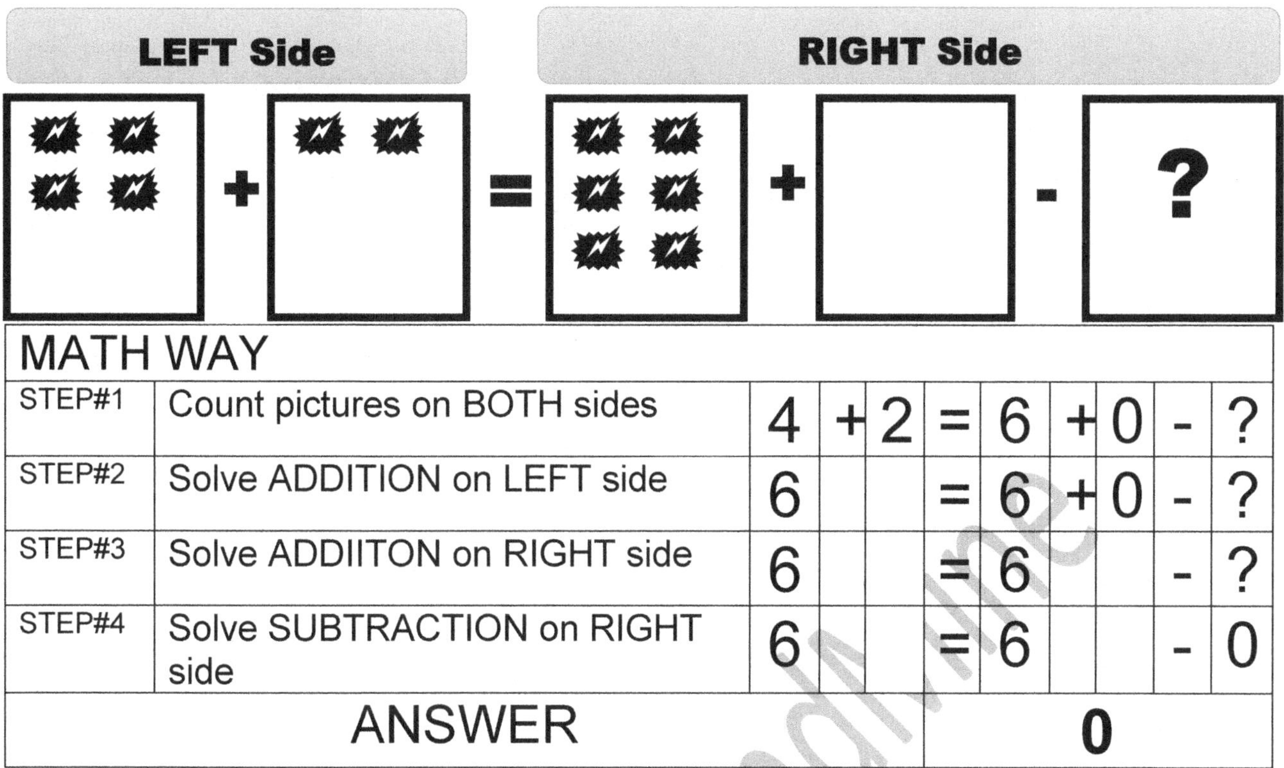

MATH WAY									
STEP#1	Count pictures on BOTH sides	4	+	2	=	6	+0	-	?
STEP#2	Solve ADDITION on LEFT side	6			=	6	+0	-	?
STEP#3	Solve ADDIITON on RIGHT side	6			=	6		-	?
STEP#4	Solve SUBTRACTION on RIGHT side	6			=	6		-	0
ANSWER						**0**			

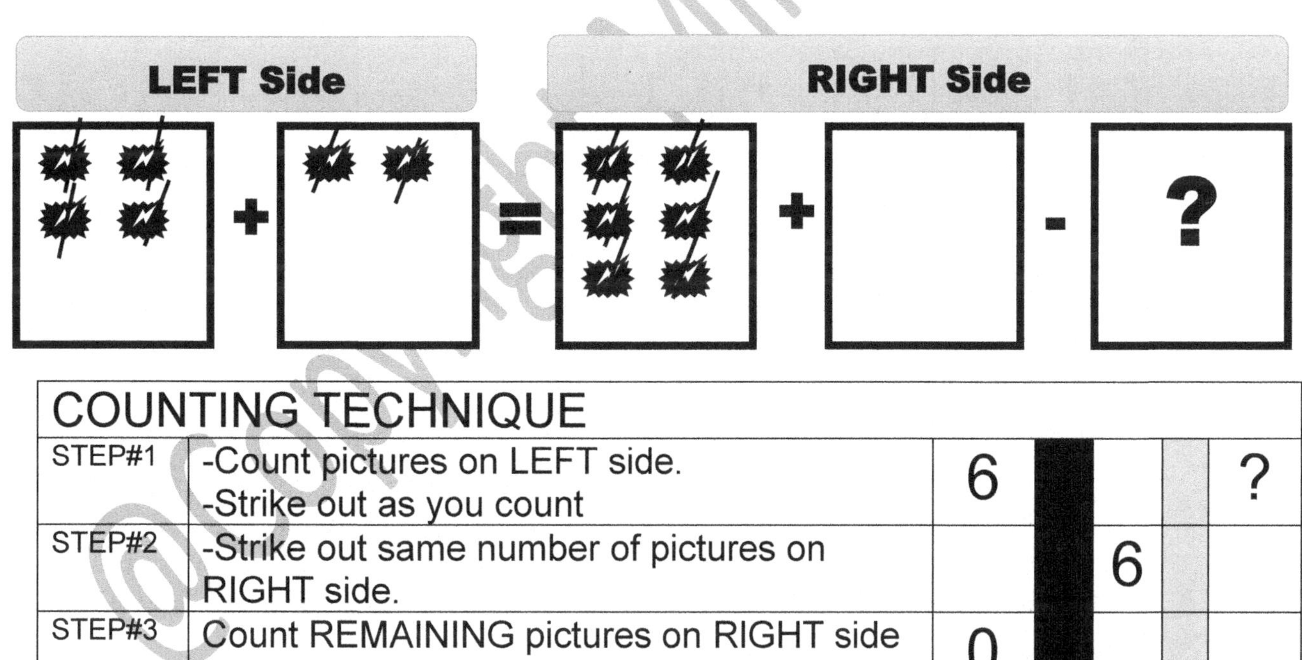

COUNTING TECHNIQUE						
STEP#1	-Count pictures on LEFT side. -Strike out as you count	6				?
STEP#2	-Strike out same number of pictures on RIGHT side.			6		
STEP#3	Count REMAINING pictures on RIGHT side	0				
ANSWER						0

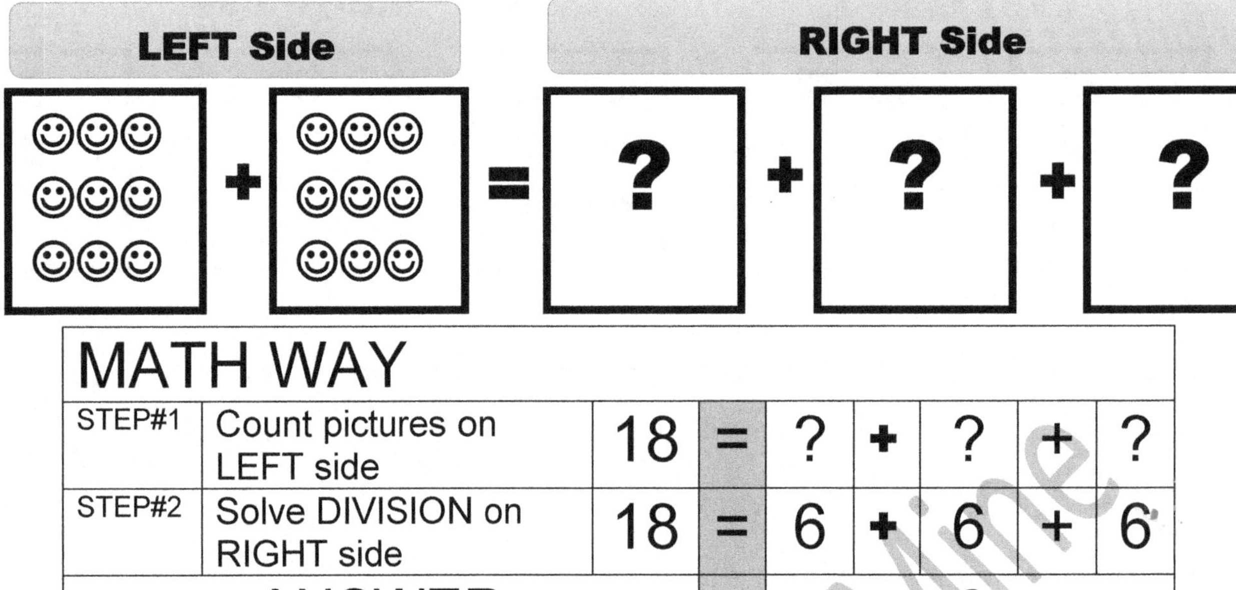

MATH WAY								
STEP#1	Count pictures on LEFT side	18	=	?	+	?	+	?
STEP#2	Solve DIVISION on RIGHT side	18	=	6	+	6	+	6
ANSWER				6				

It is good to know:

1	+	1	+	1	=	3
2	+	2	+	2	=	6
3	+	3	+	3	=	9
4	+	4	+	4	=	12
5	+	5	+	5	=	15
6	+	6	+	6	=	18
7	+	7	+	7	=	21
8	+	8	+	8	=	24
9	+	9	+	9	=	27
10	+	10	+	10	=	30

Question 1

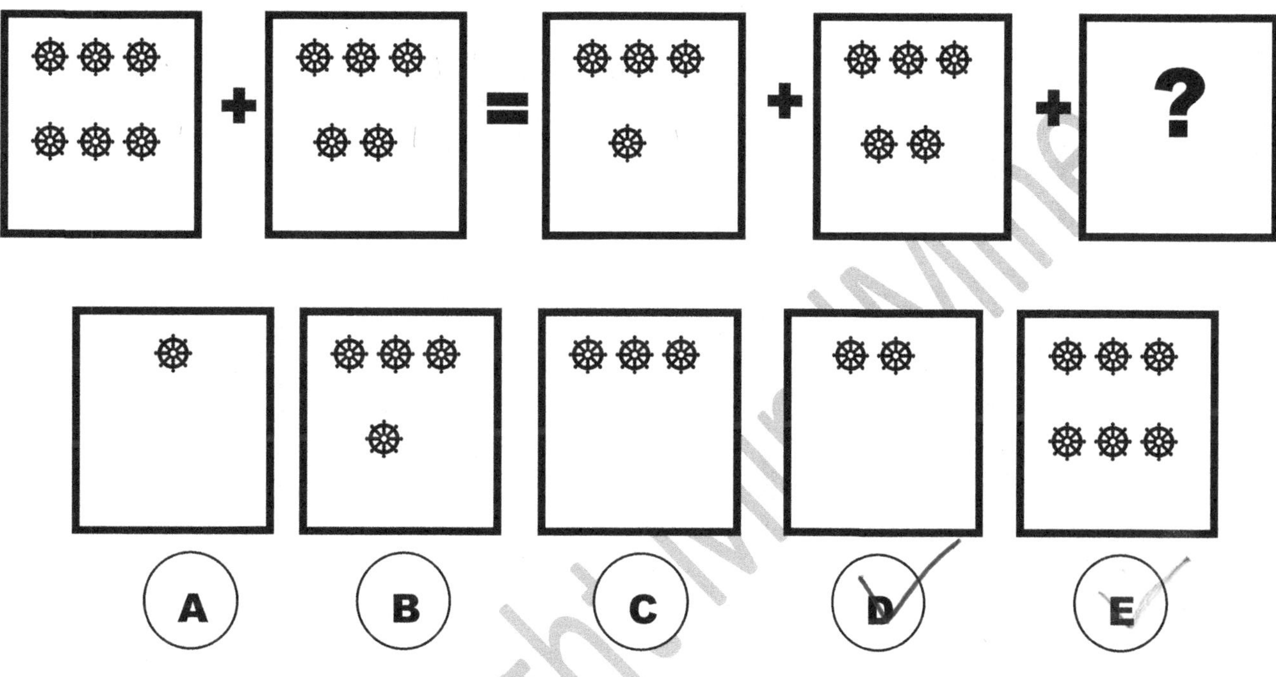

Question 2

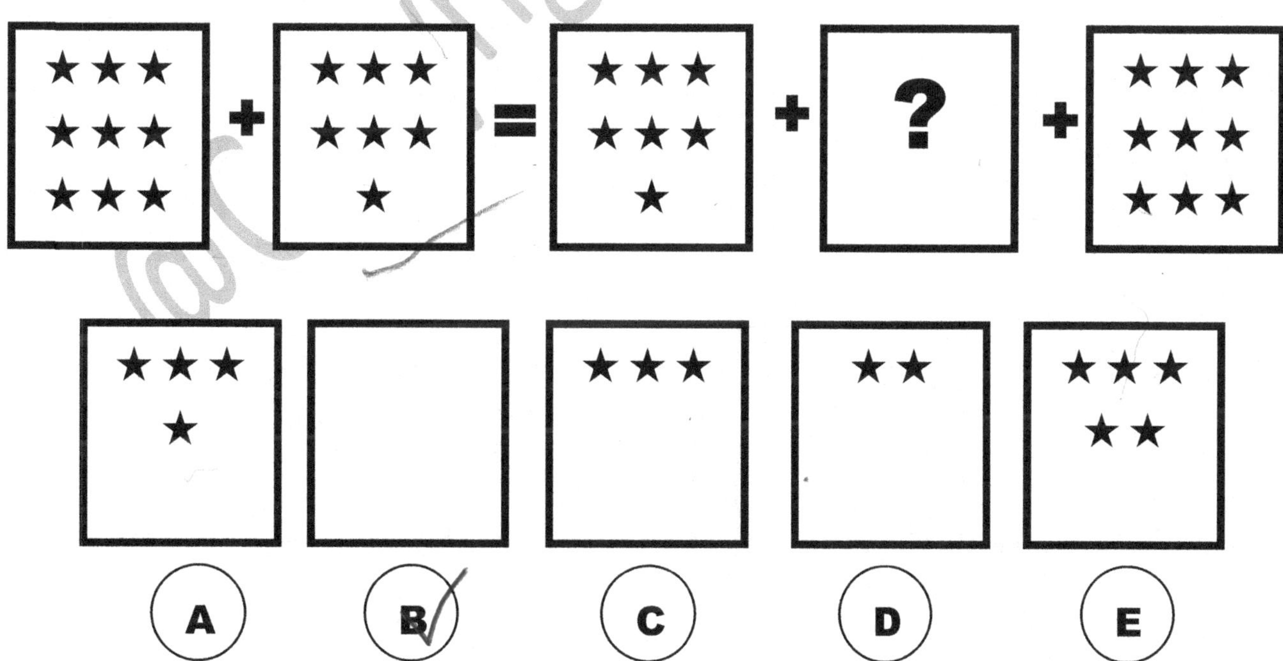

Question 3

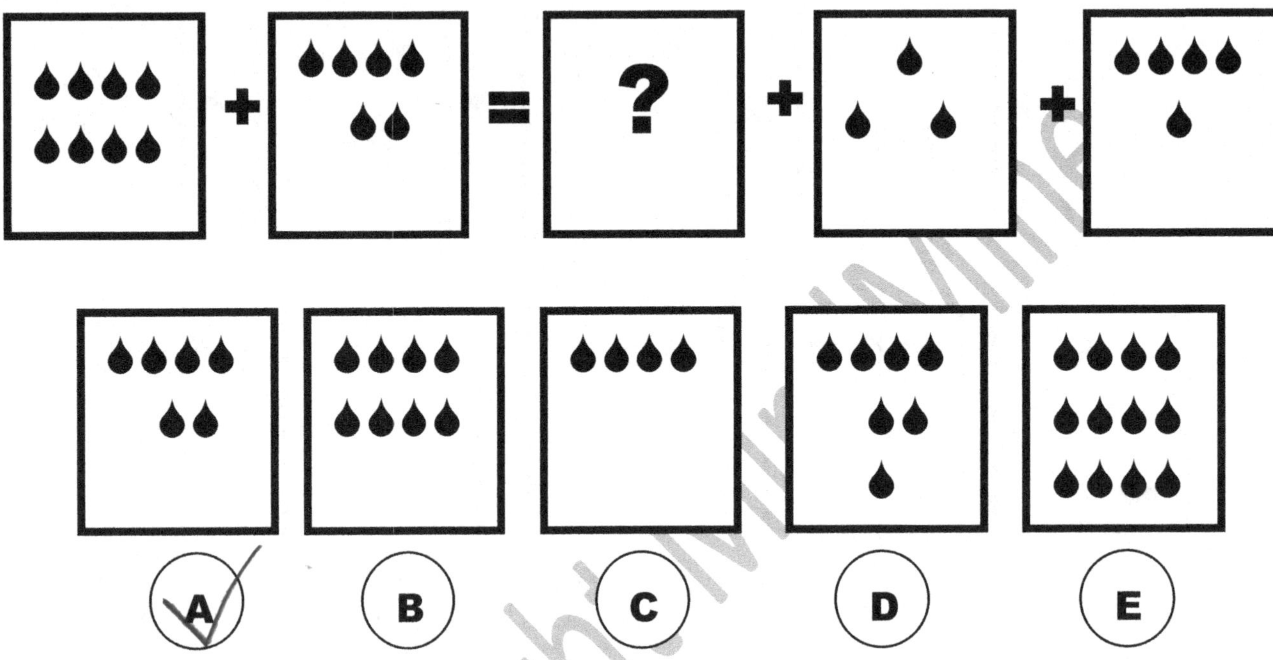

Question 4

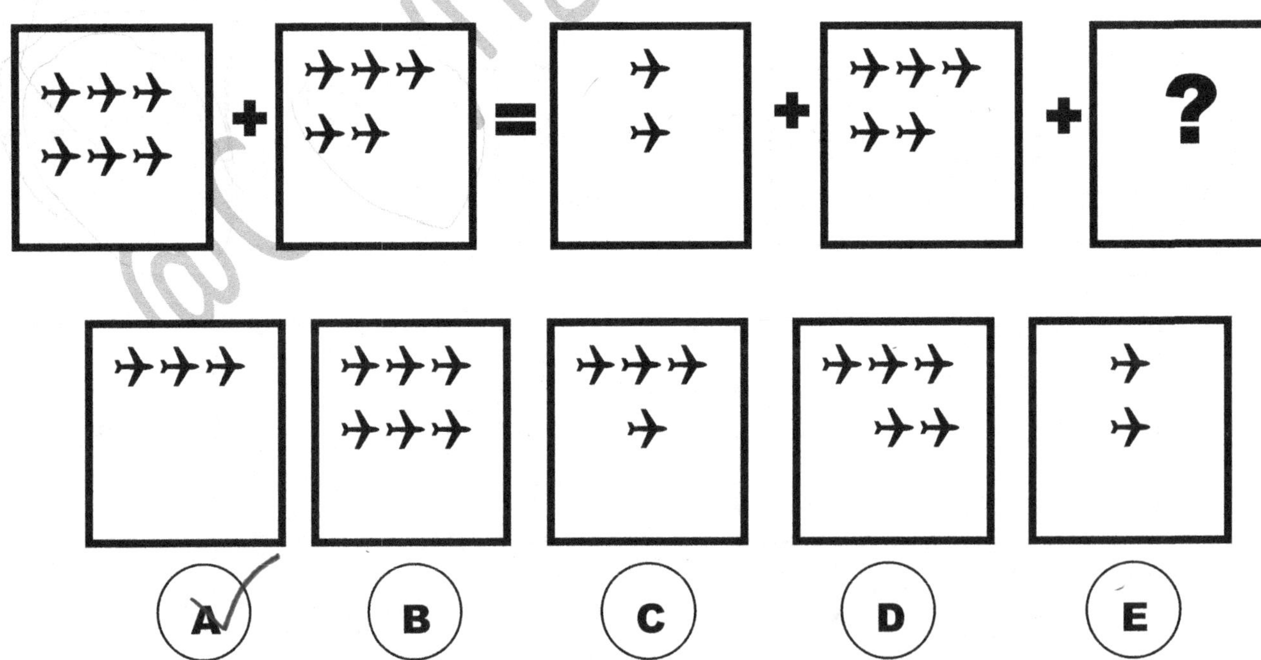

Question 5

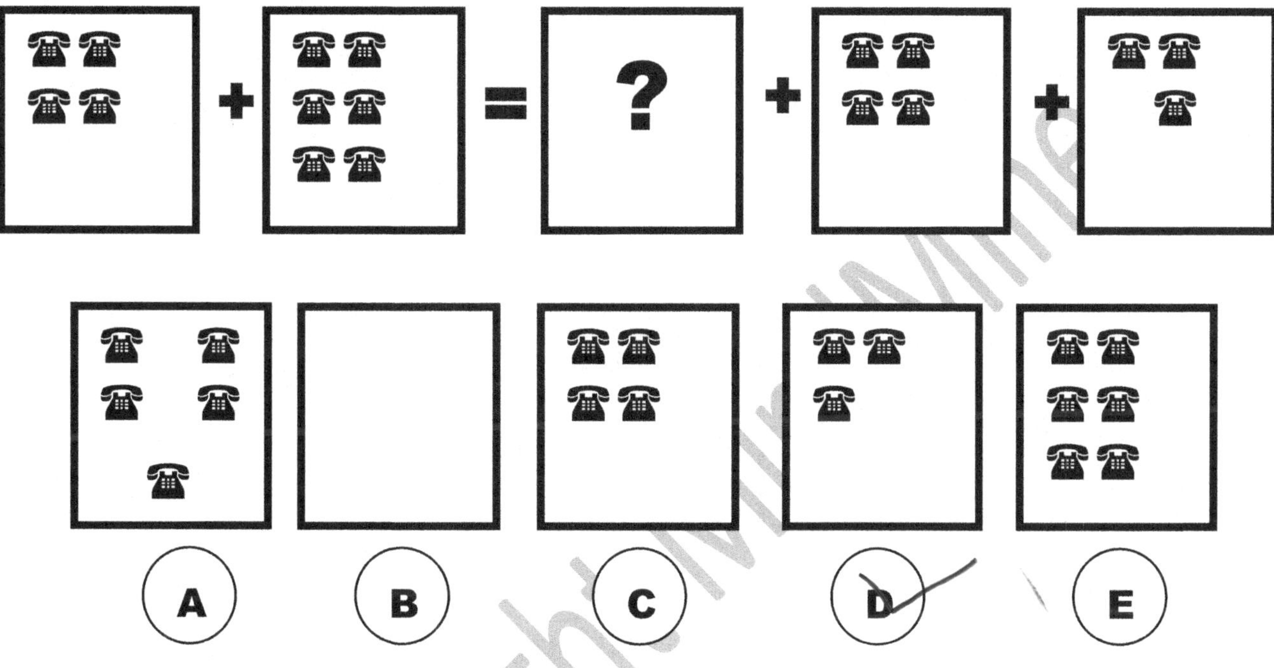

Question 6

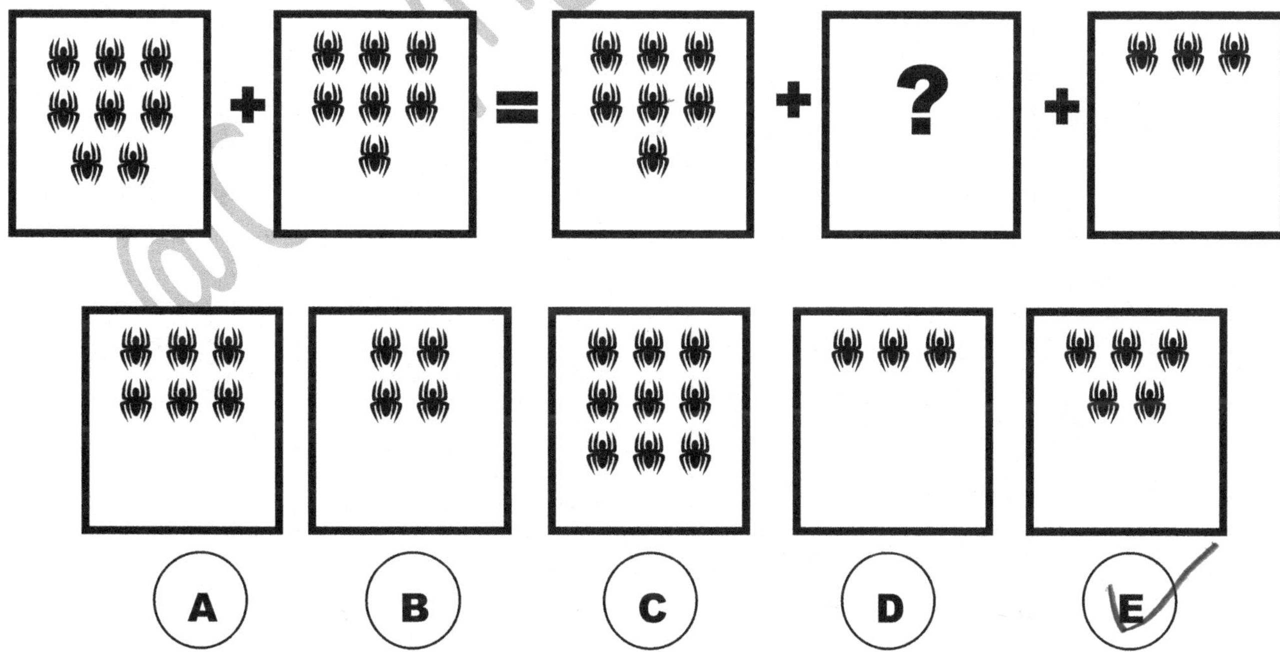

Question 7

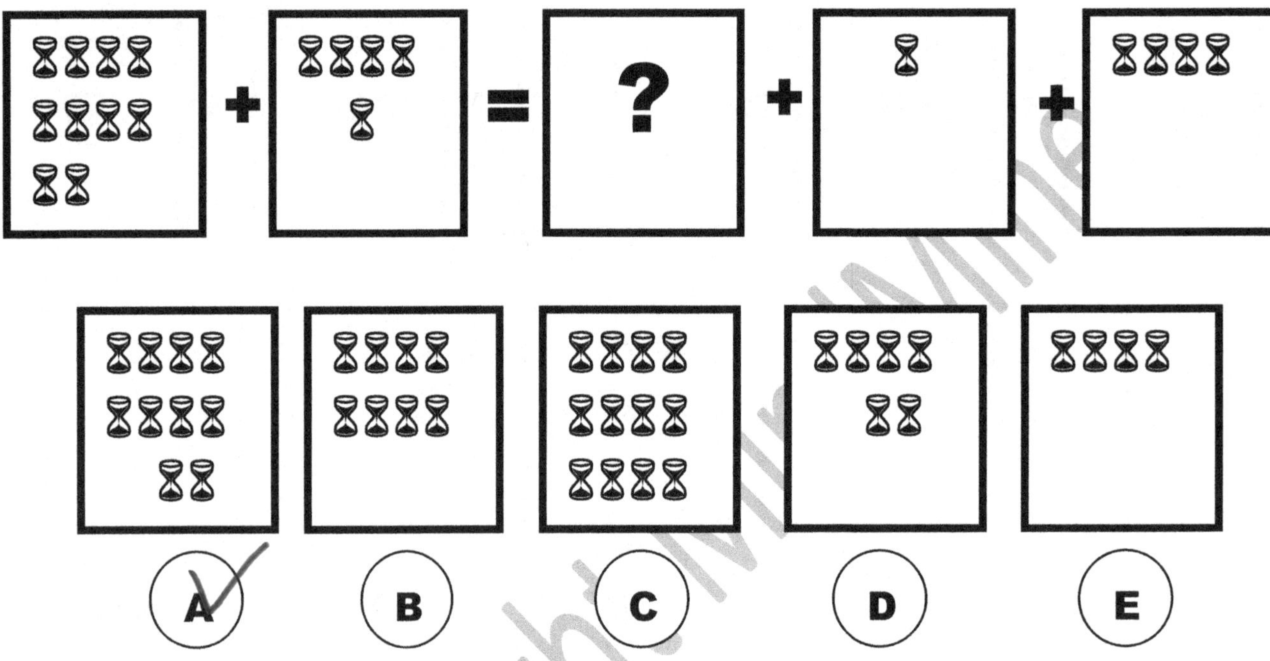

Question 8

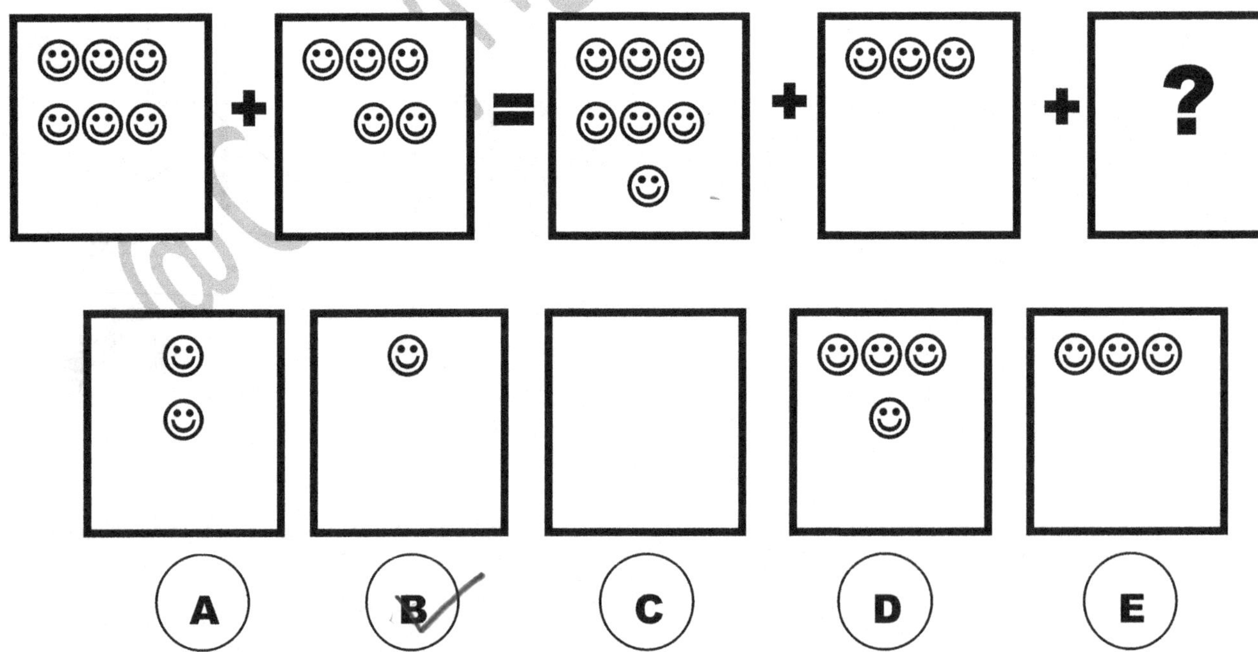

Question 9

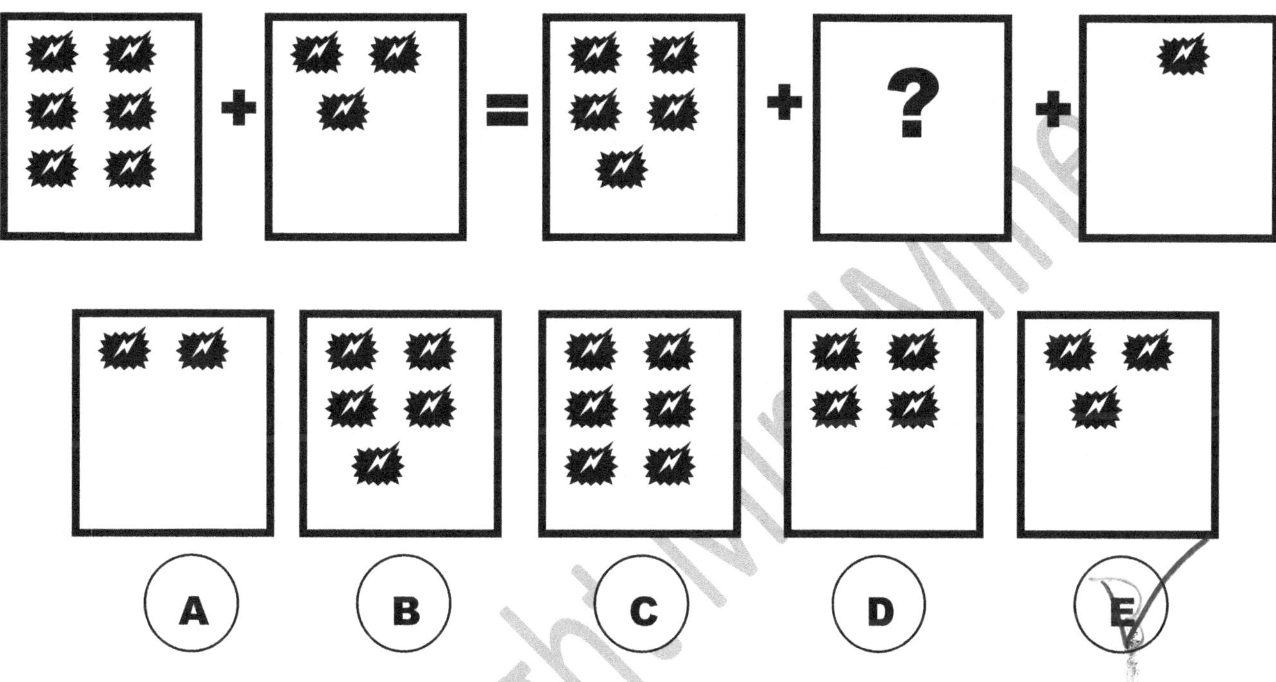

Question 10

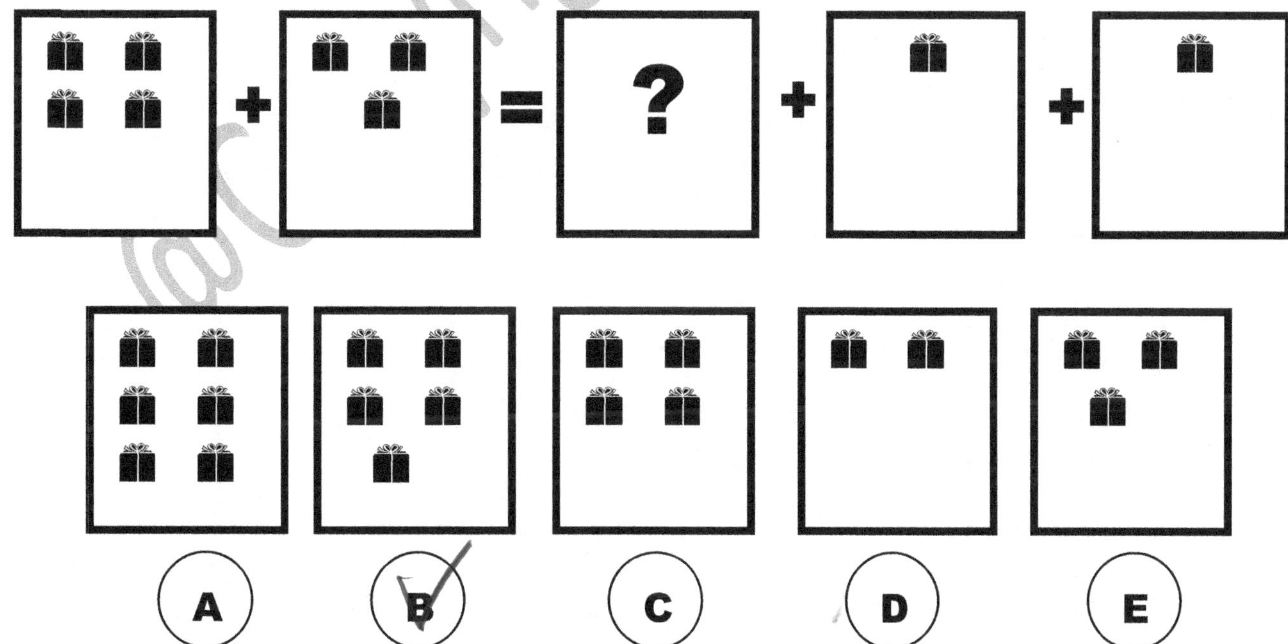

Question 11

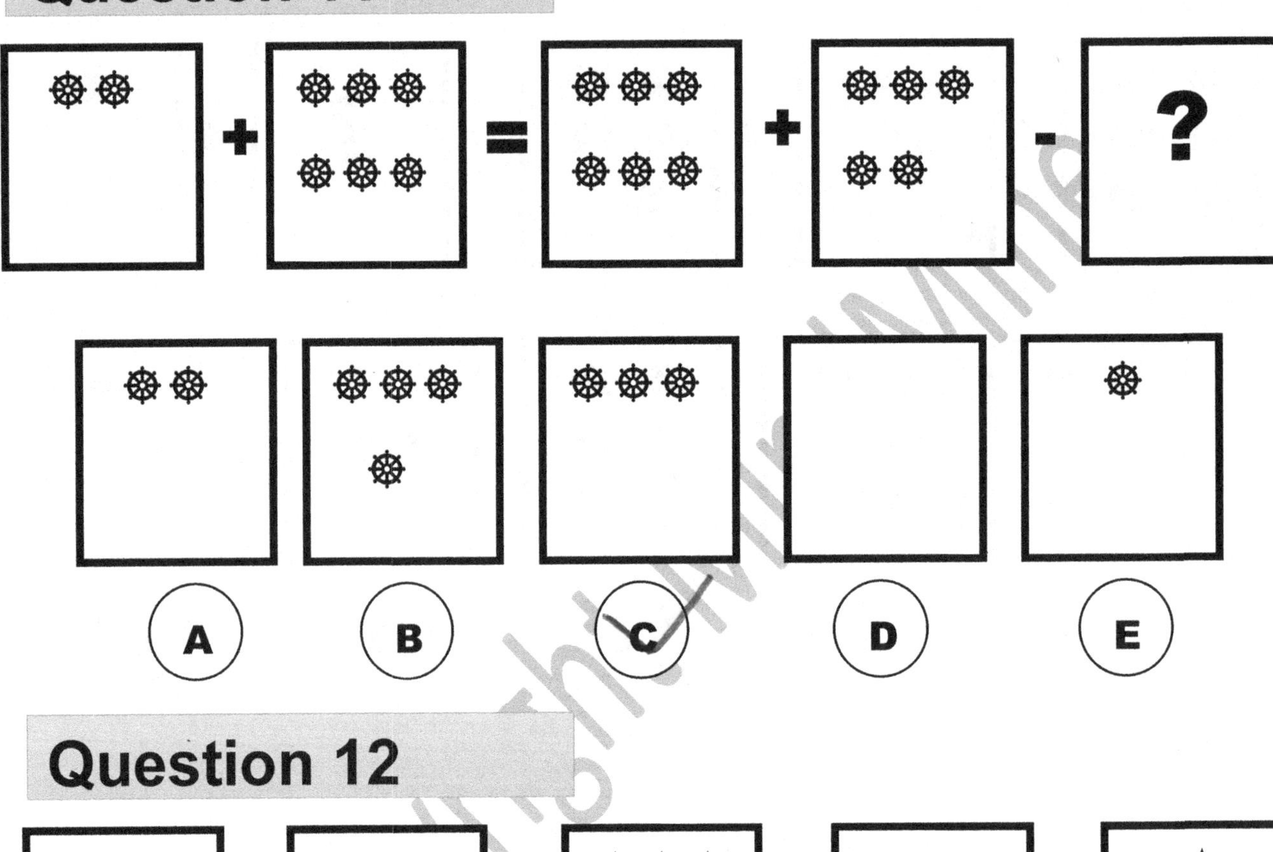

Question 12

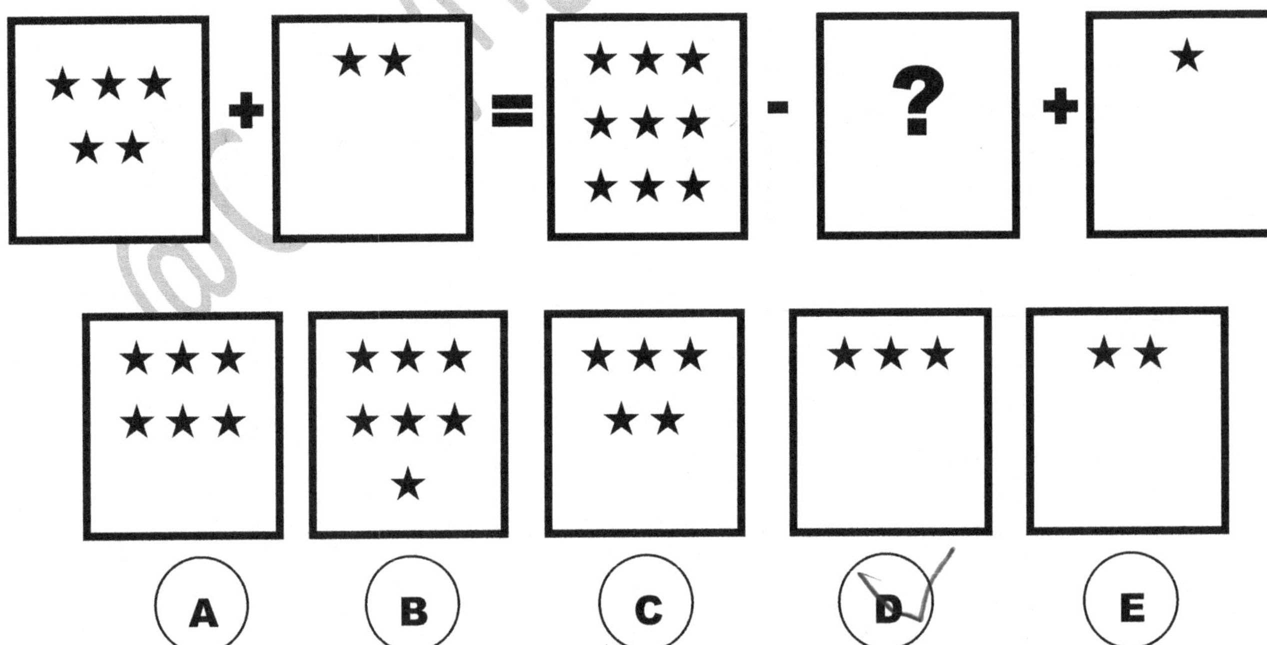

Question 13

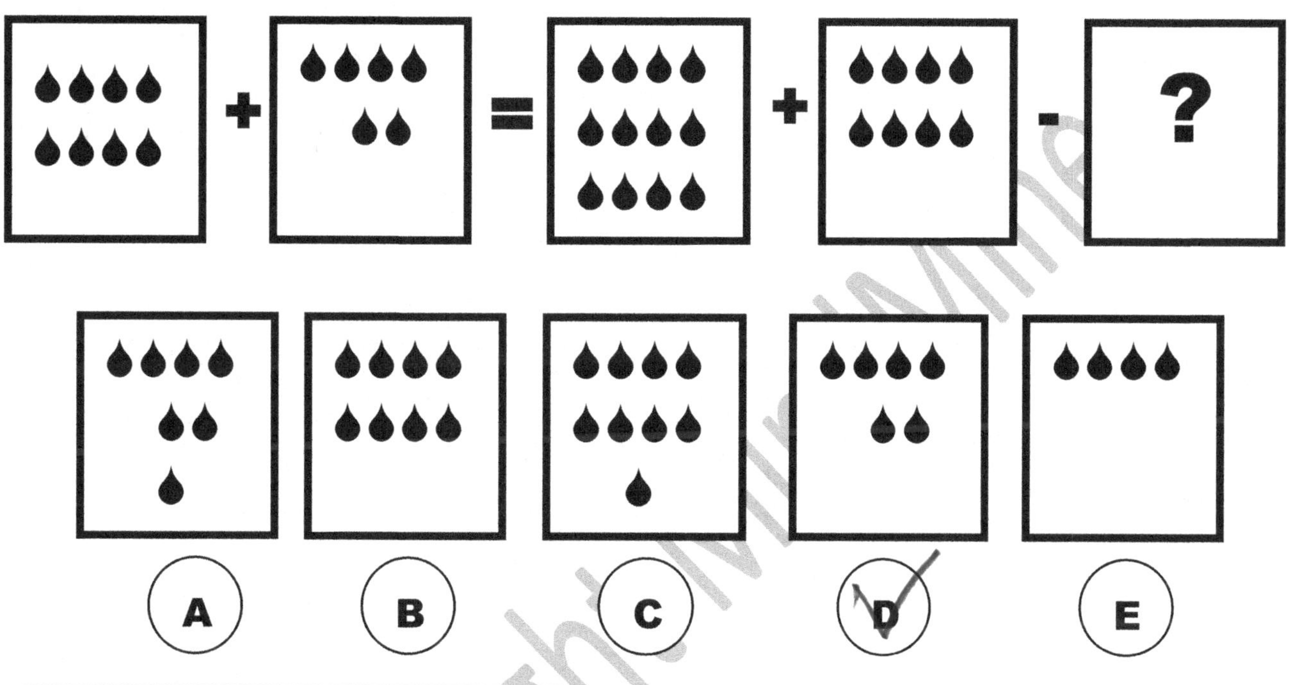

Question 14

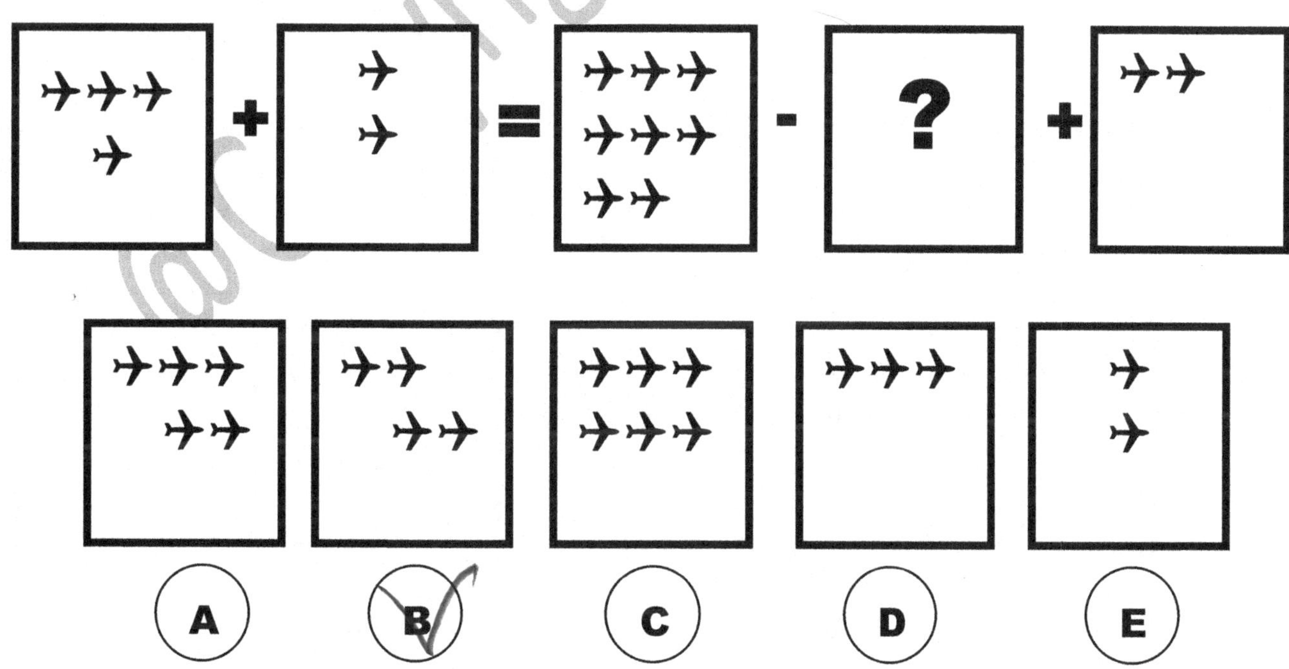

Question 15

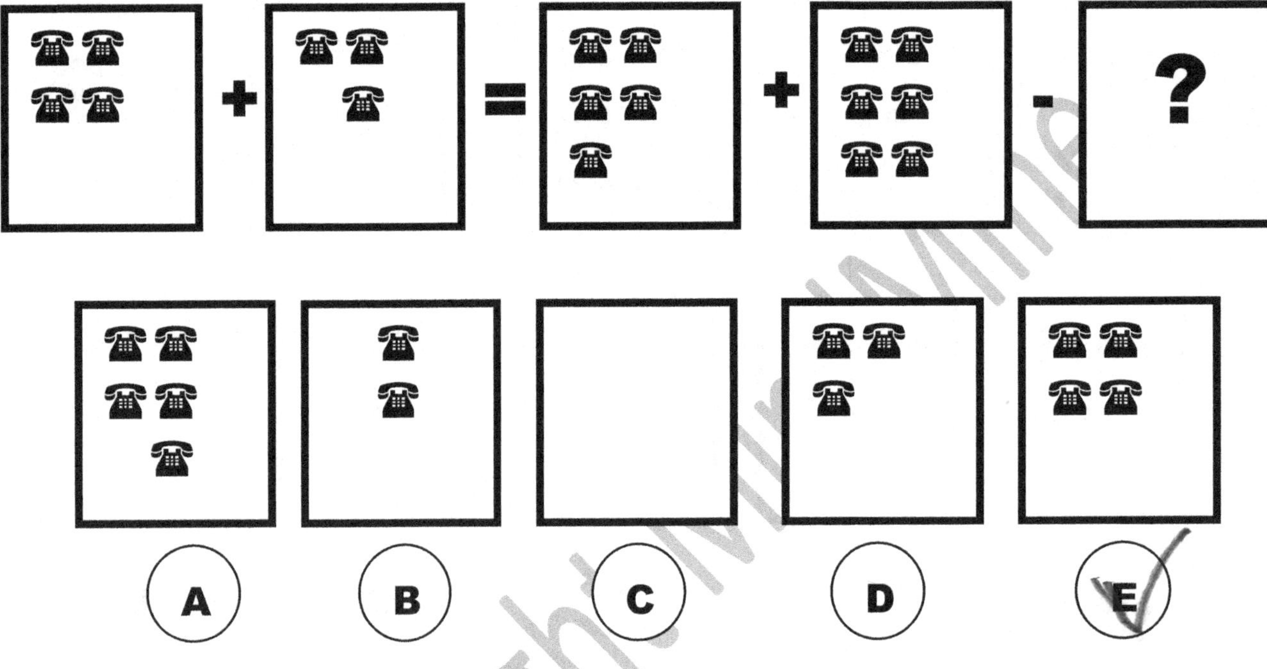

Question 16

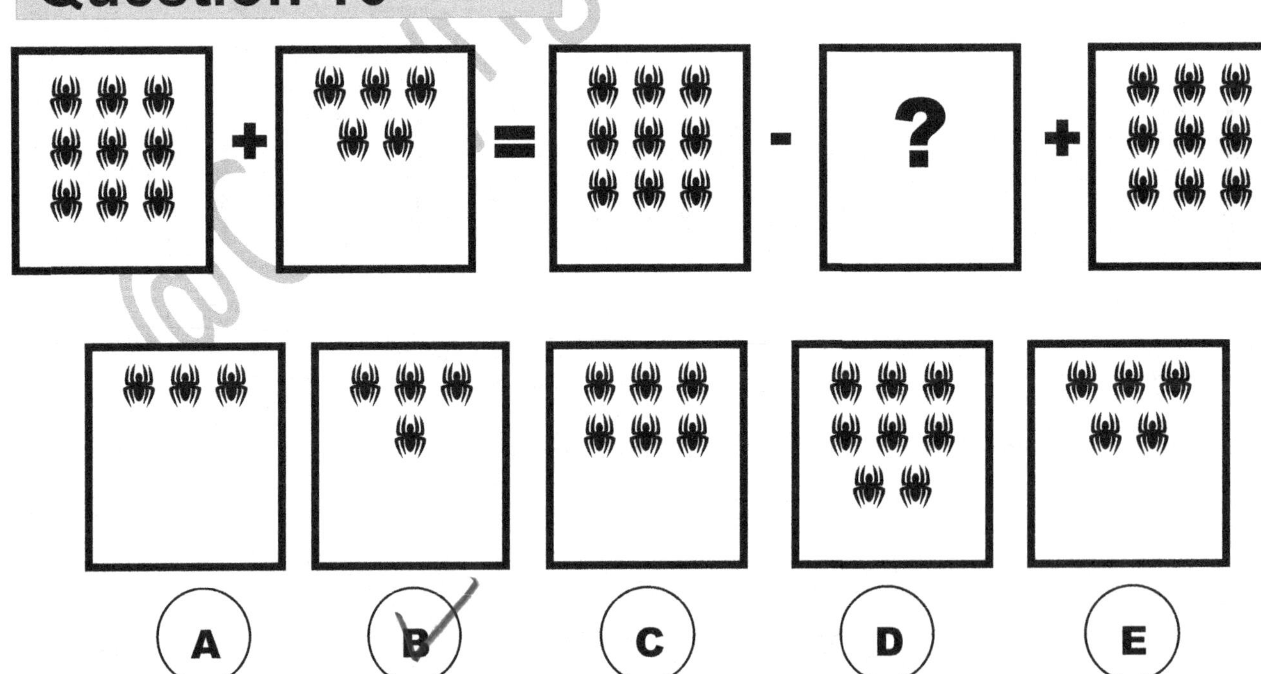

Question 17

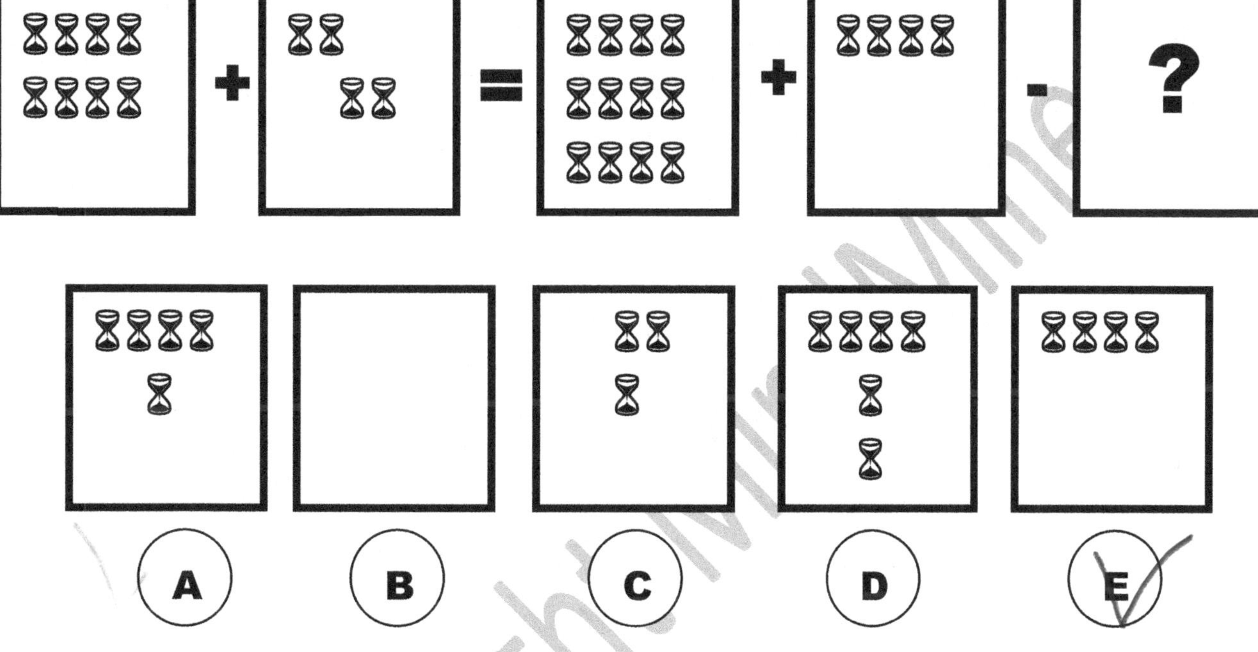

Question 18

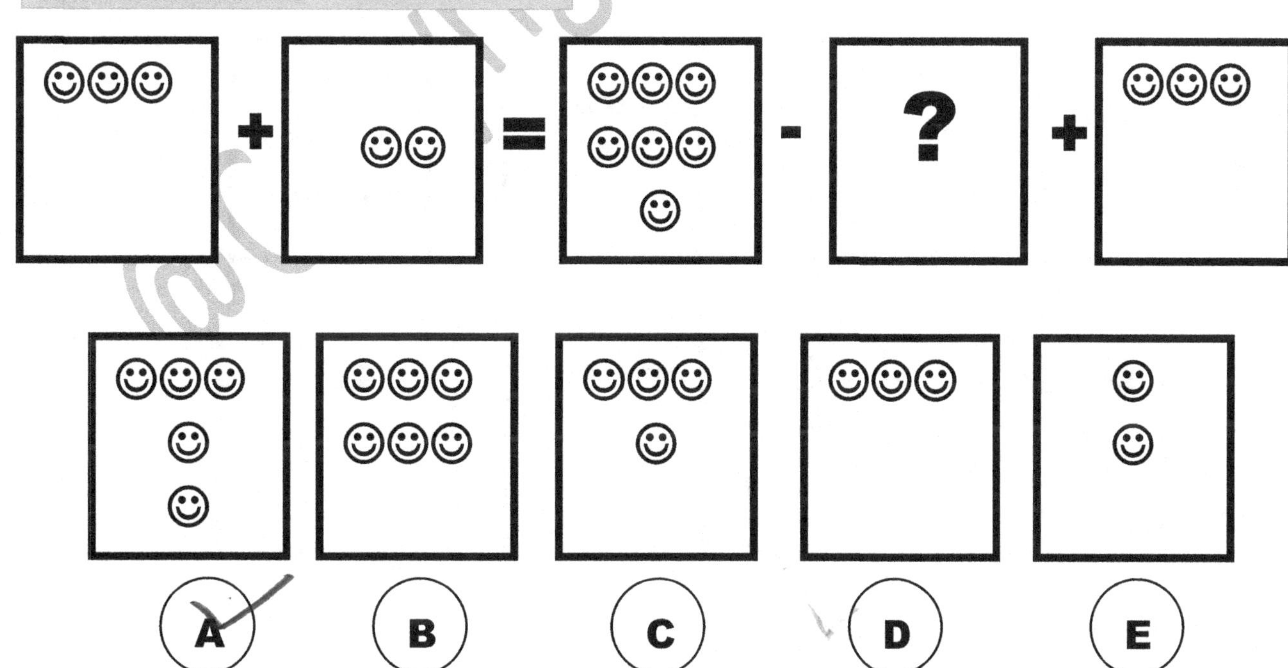

Question 19

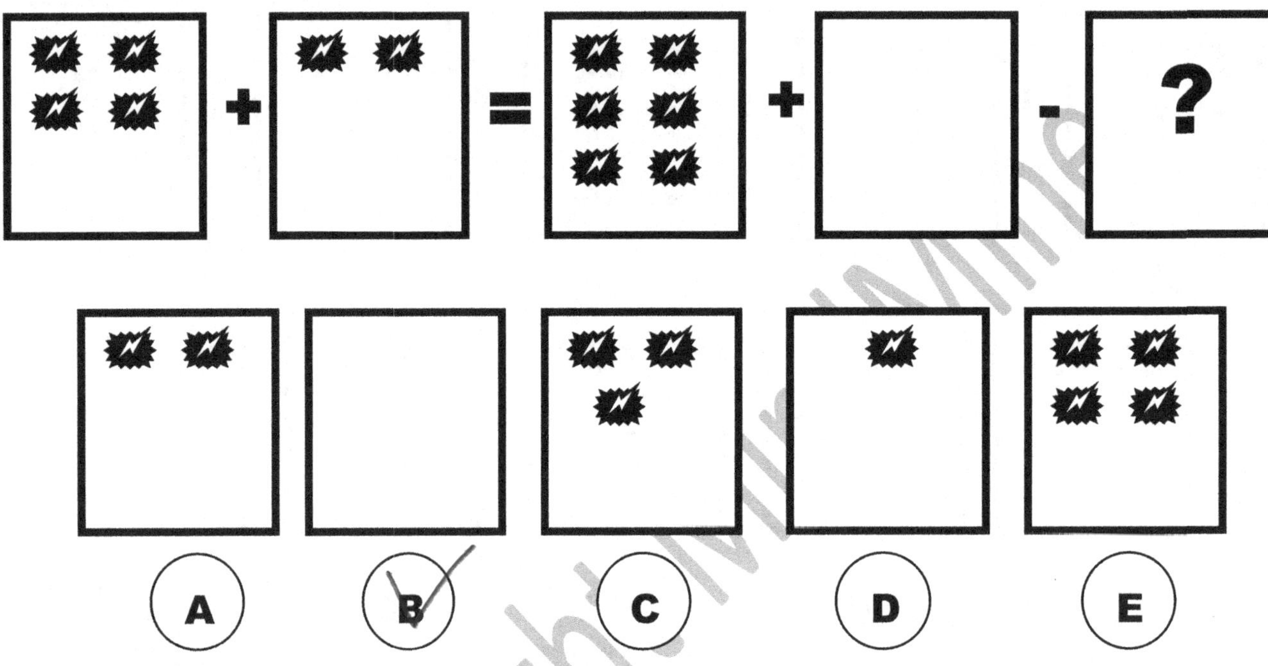

Question 20

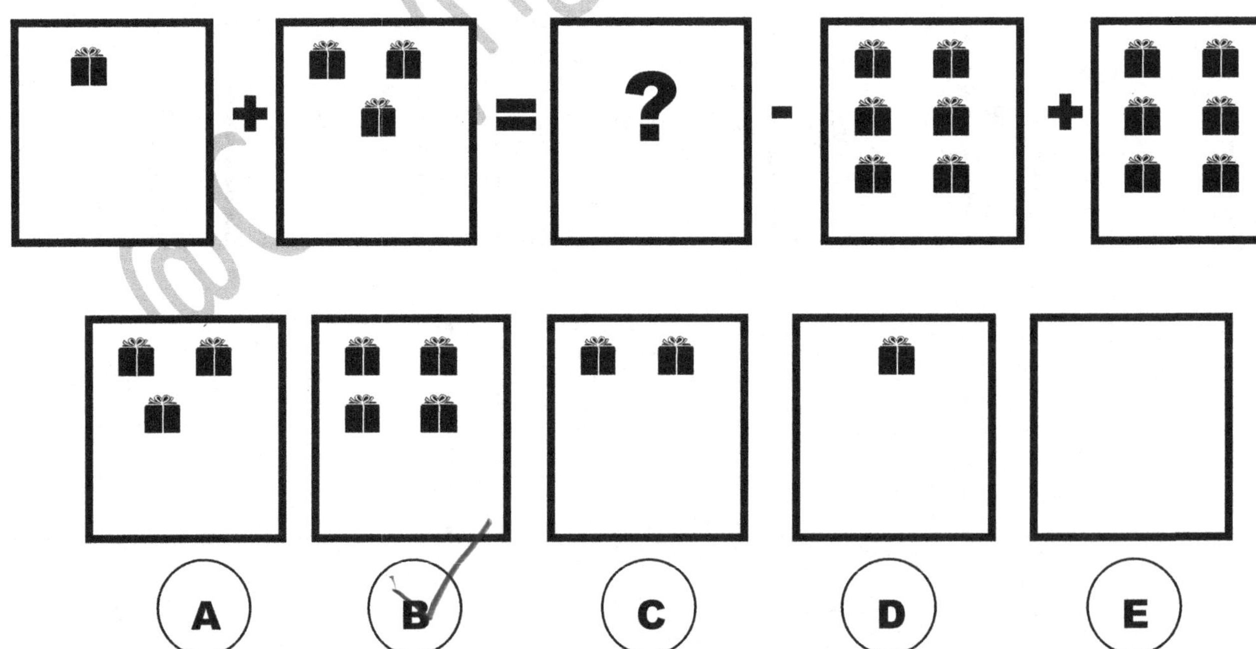

Question 21

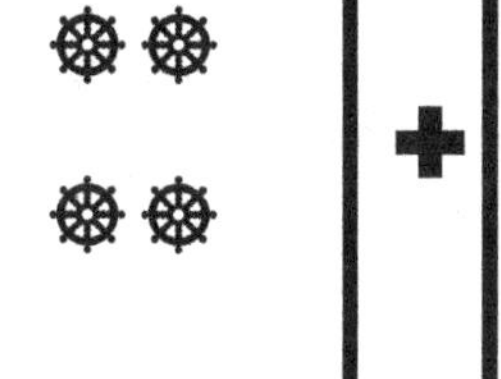

A B C D E

Question 22

A B C D E

Question 23

A B C D E

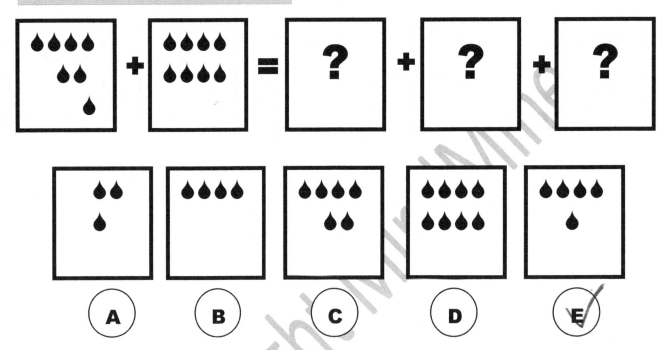

Question 24

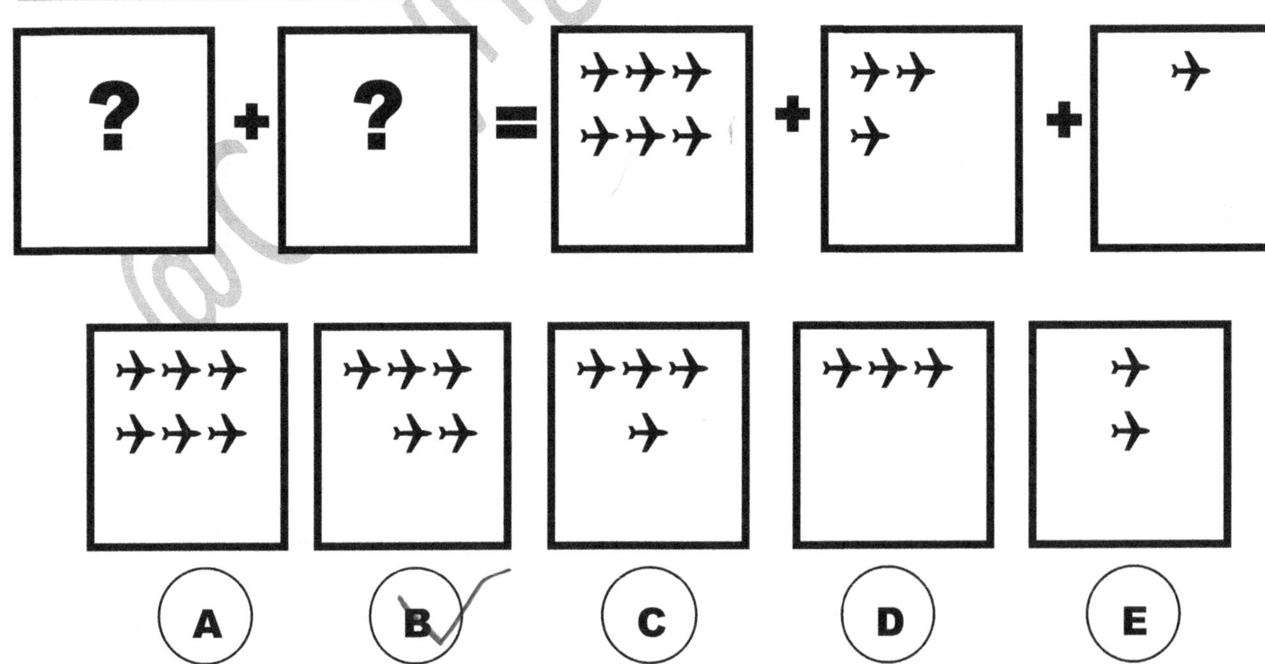

Question 25

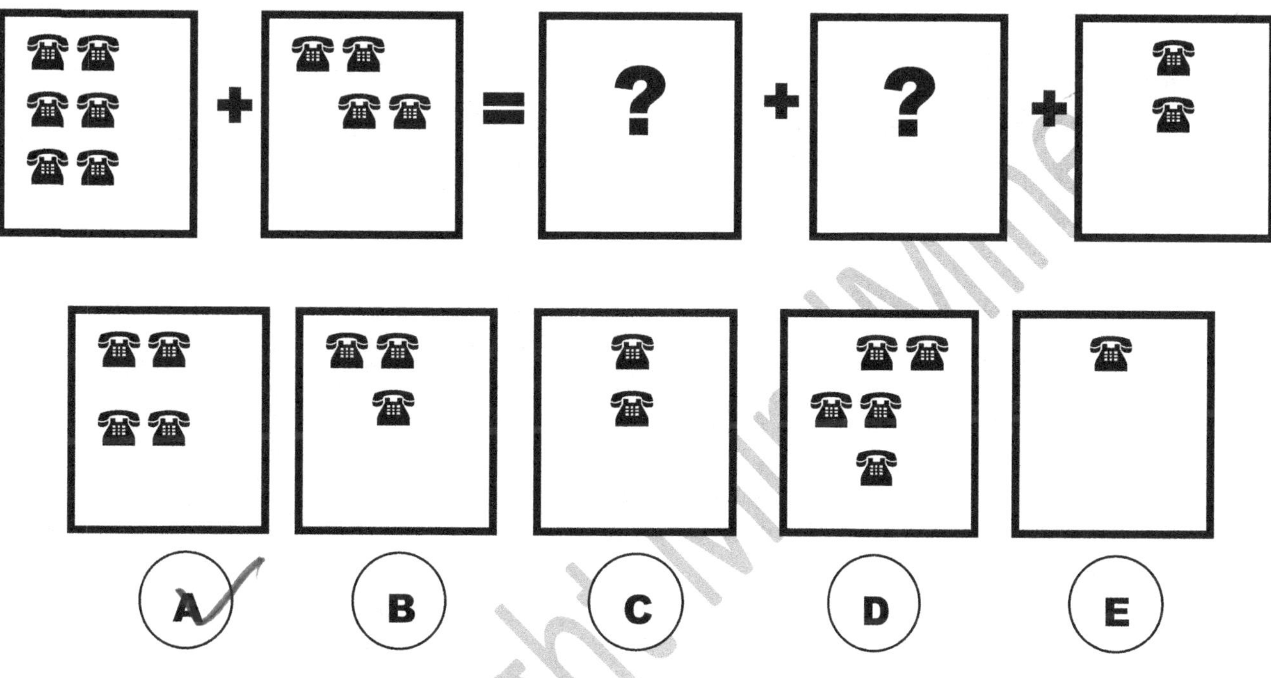

Question 26

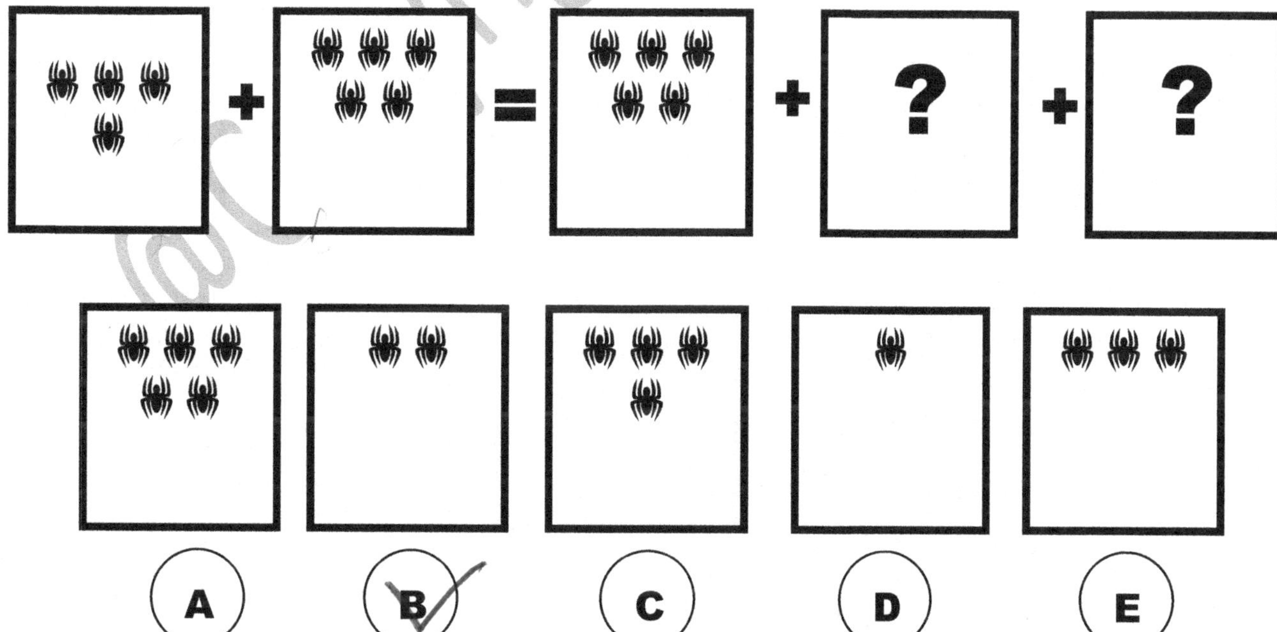

Question 27

? + ? = + +

A B C D E

Question 28

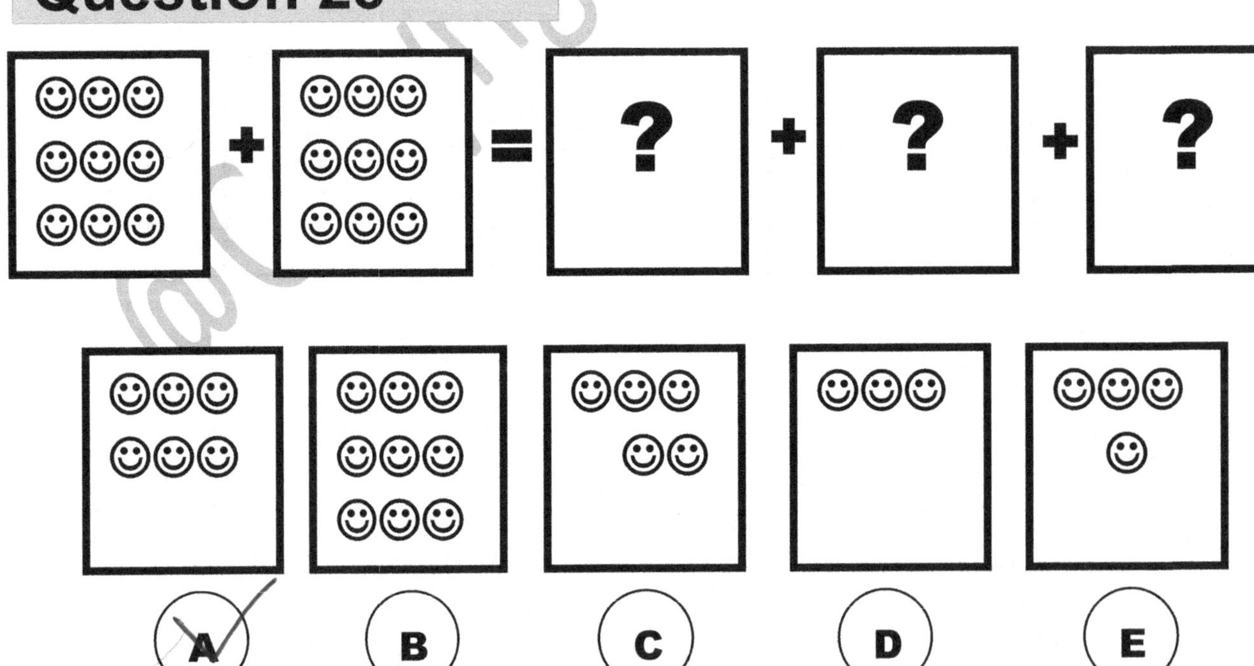

Question 29

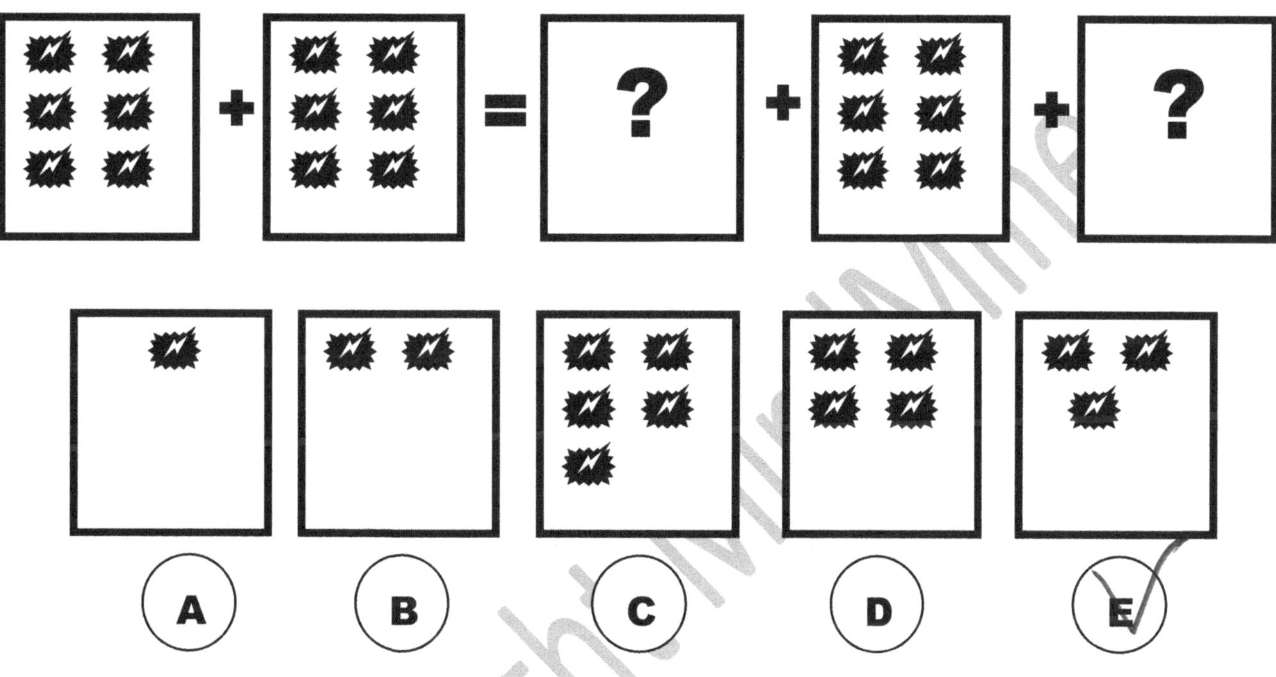

Question 30

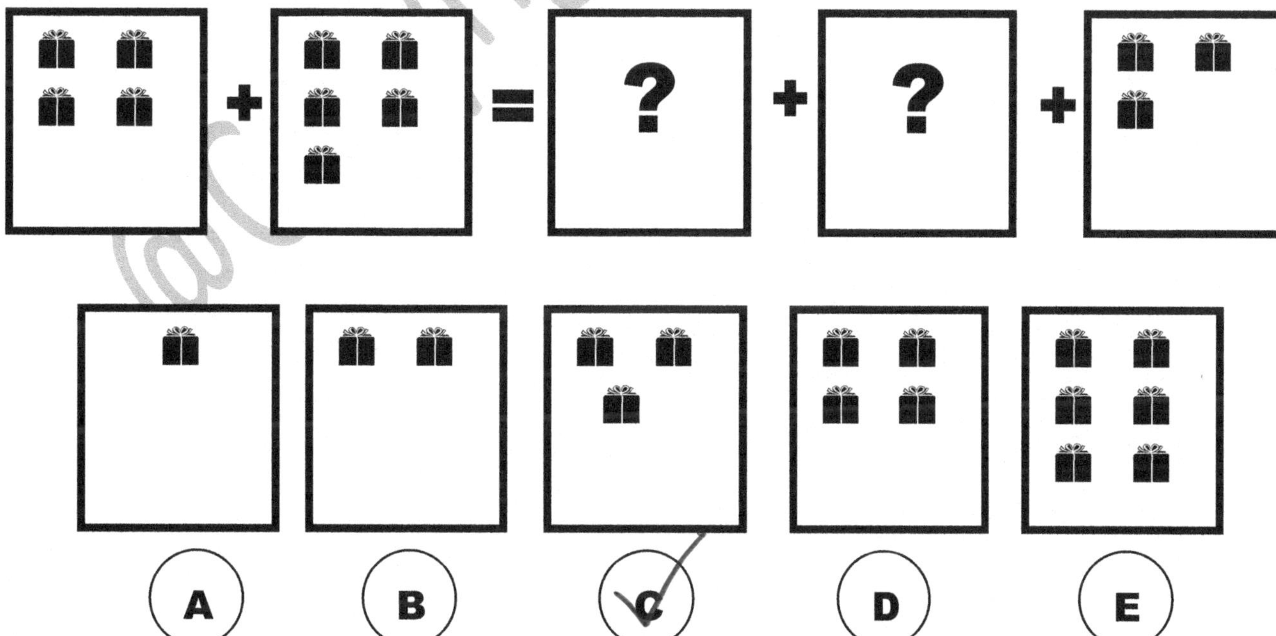

PRACTICE TEST-1

Question 1

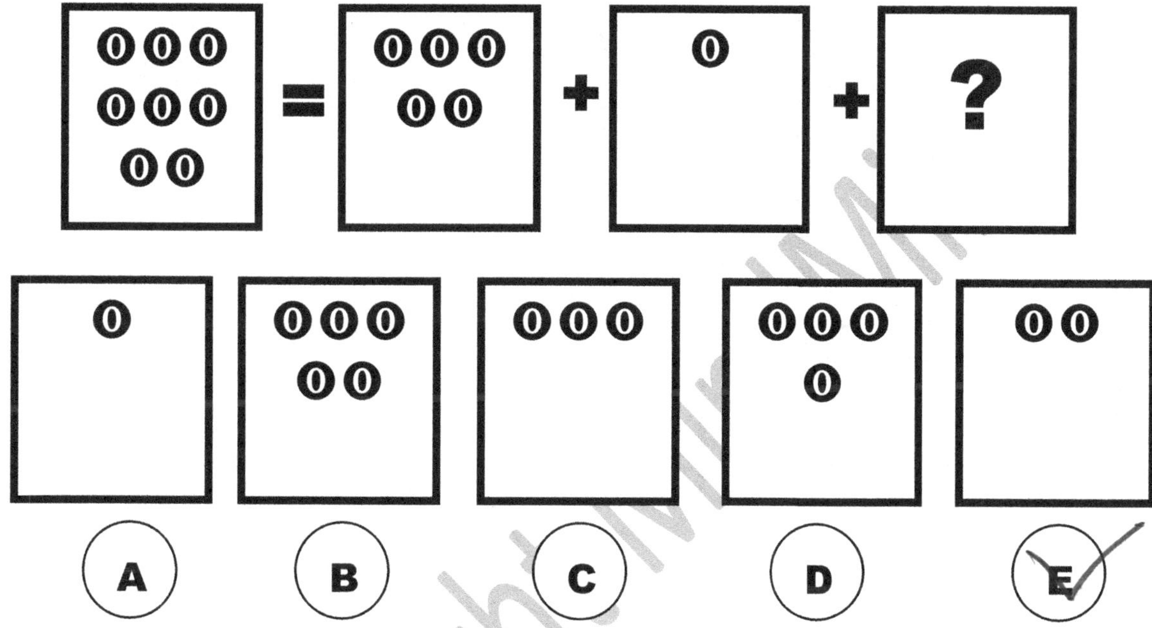

Question 2

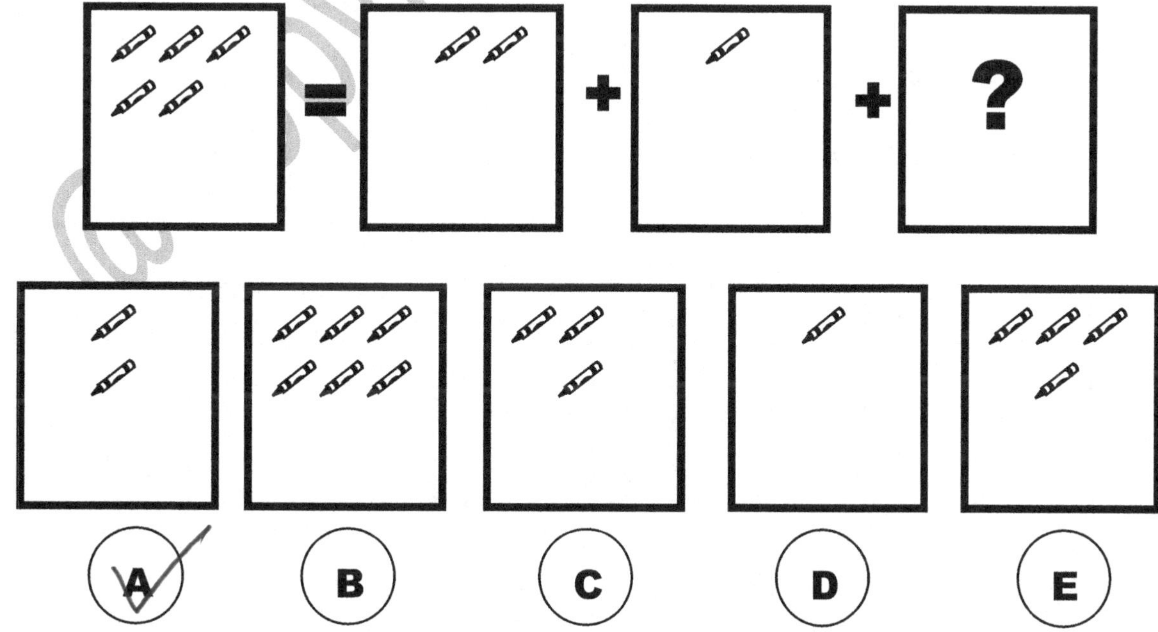

Question 3

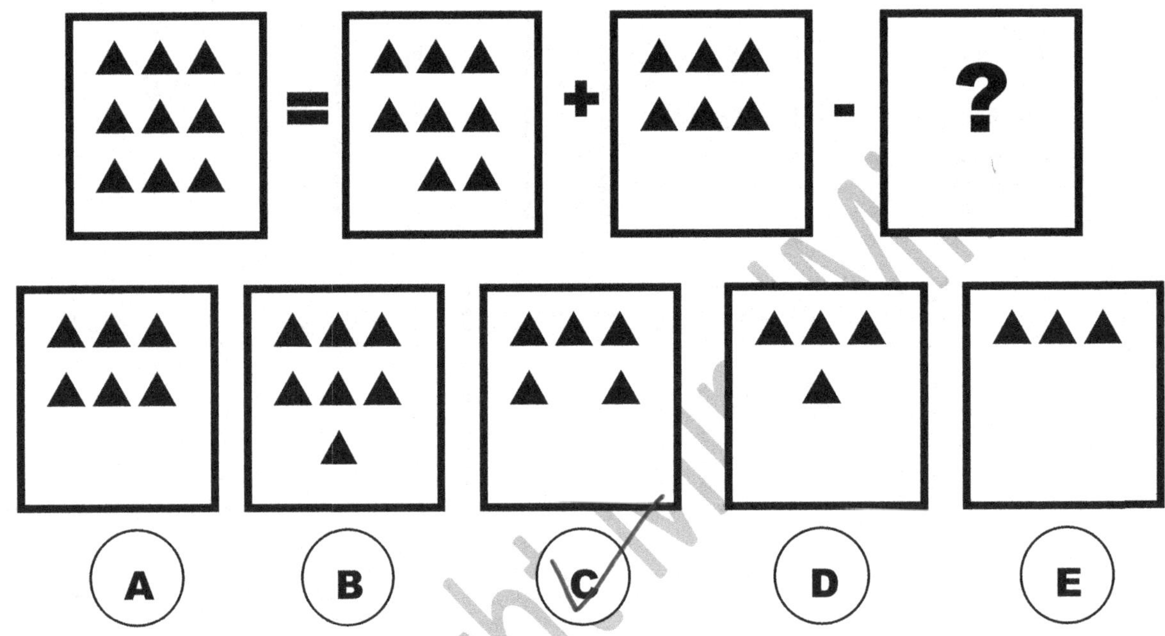

Question 4

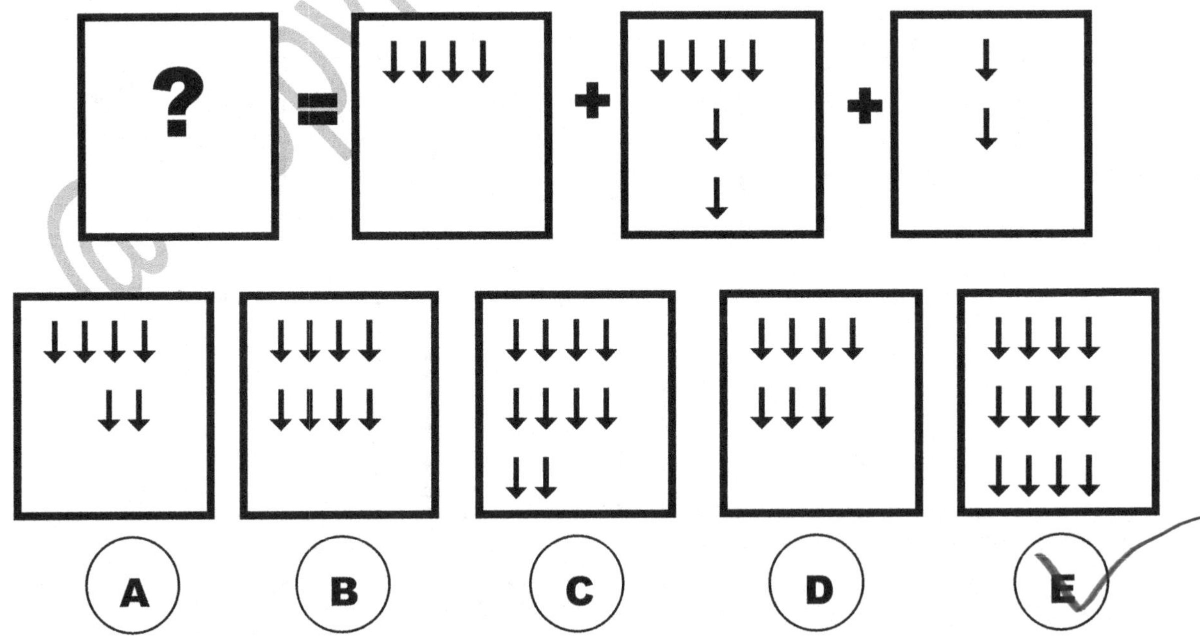

Question 5

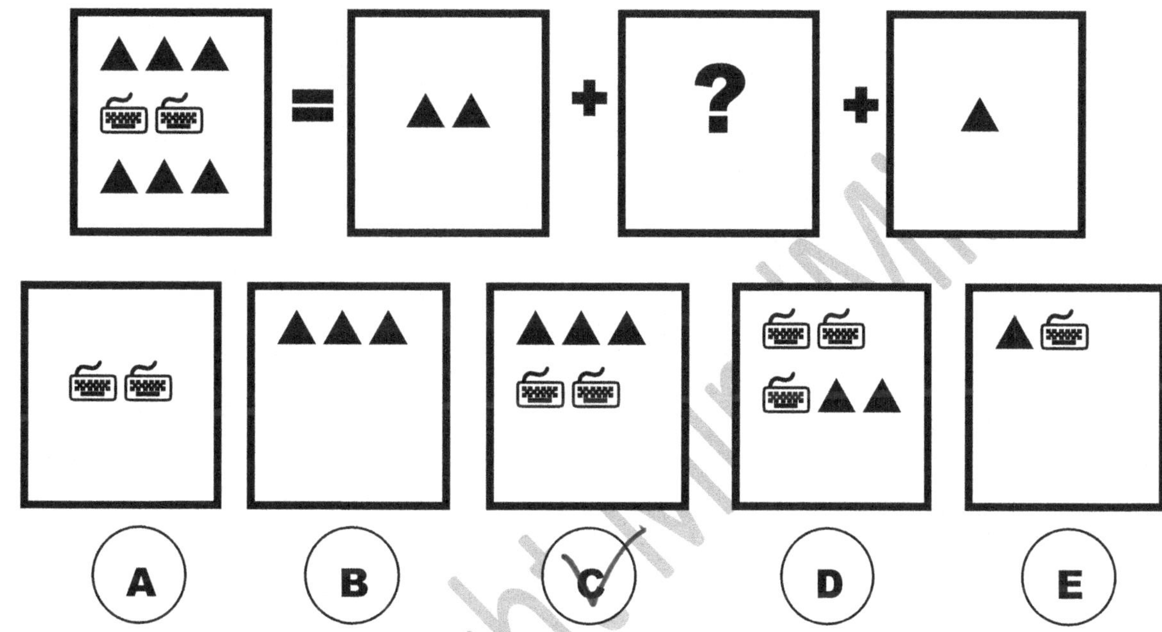

Question 6

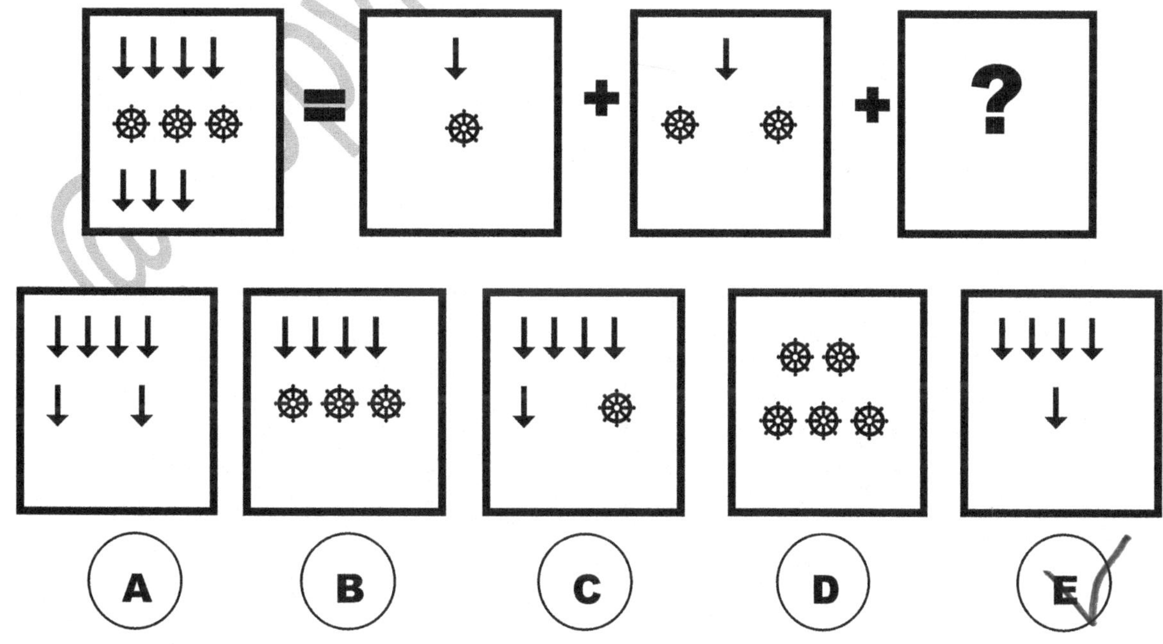

Question 7

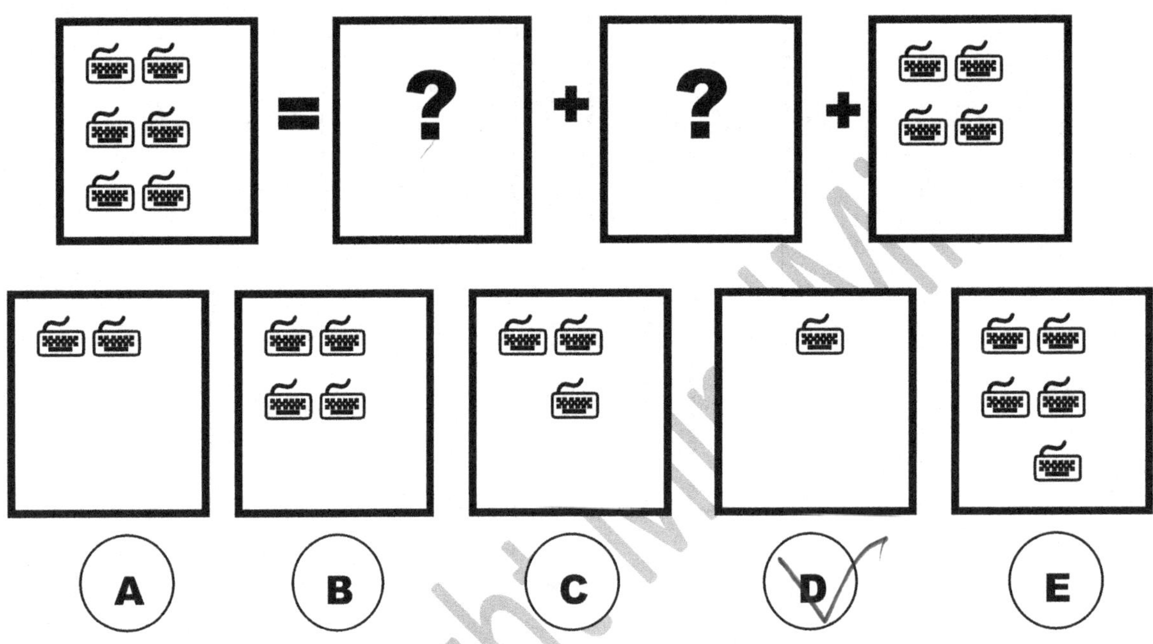

Question 8

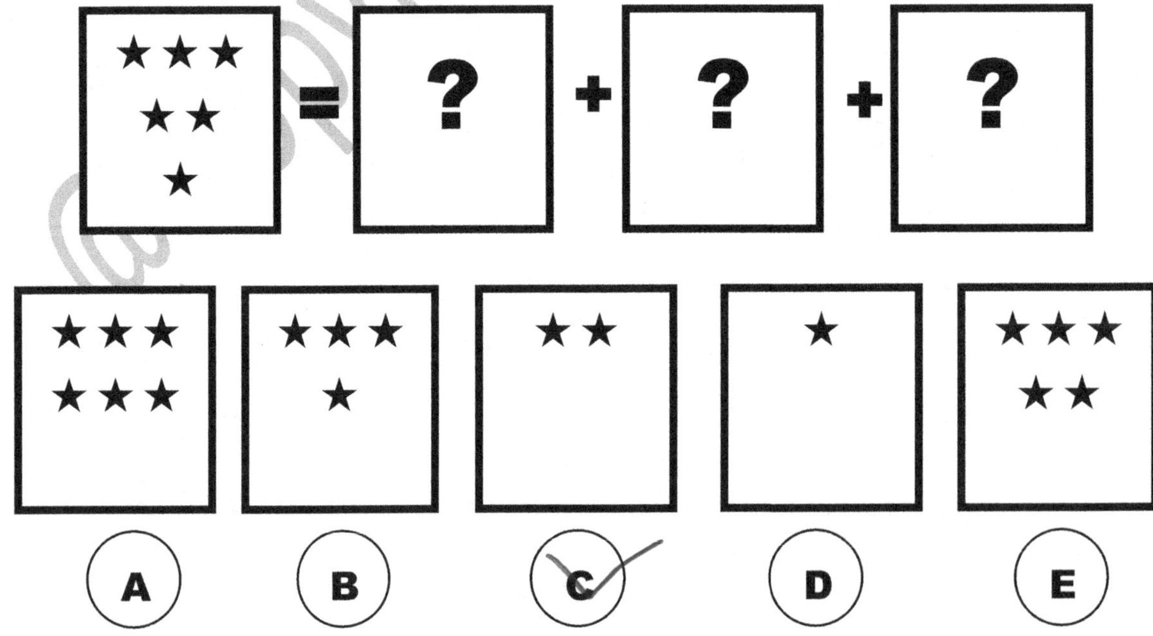

Question 9

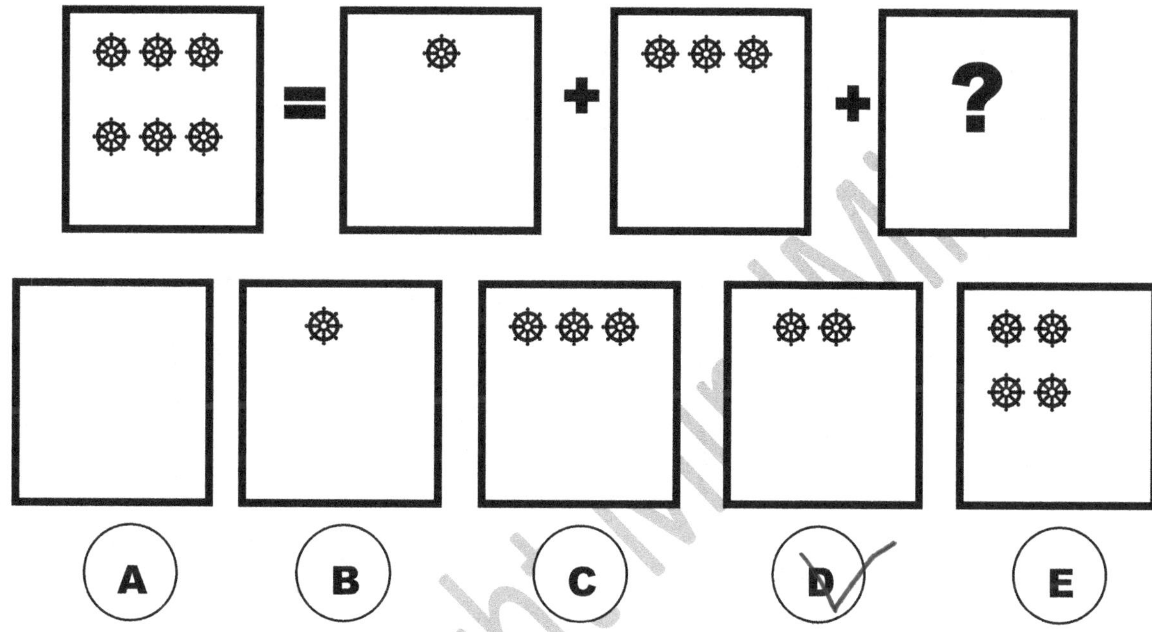

Question 10

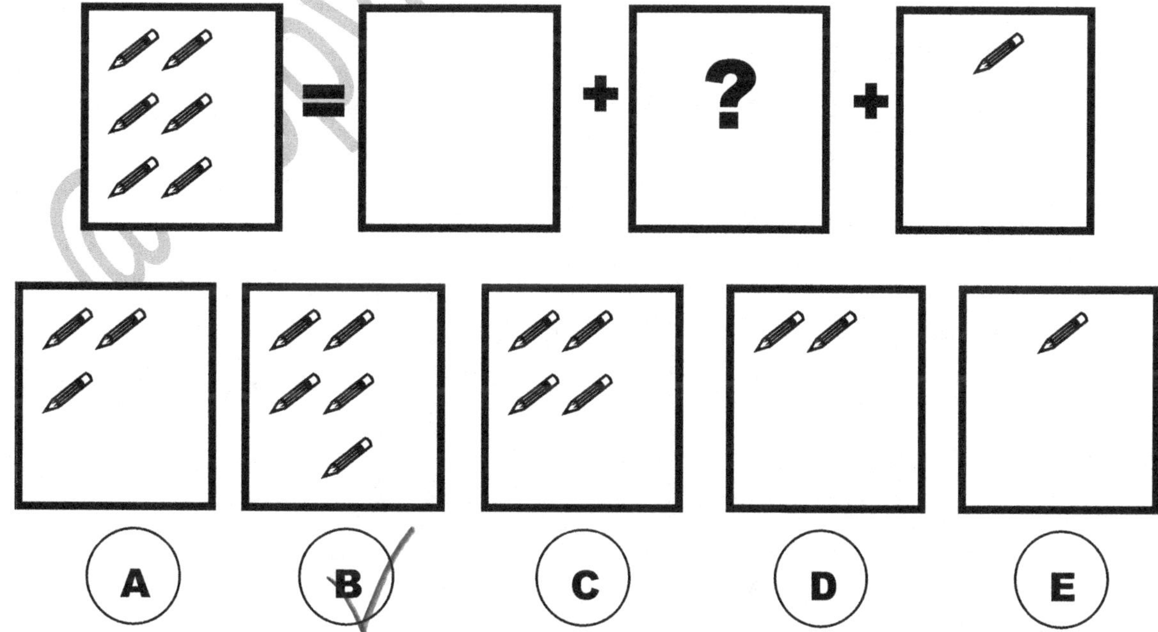

Question 11

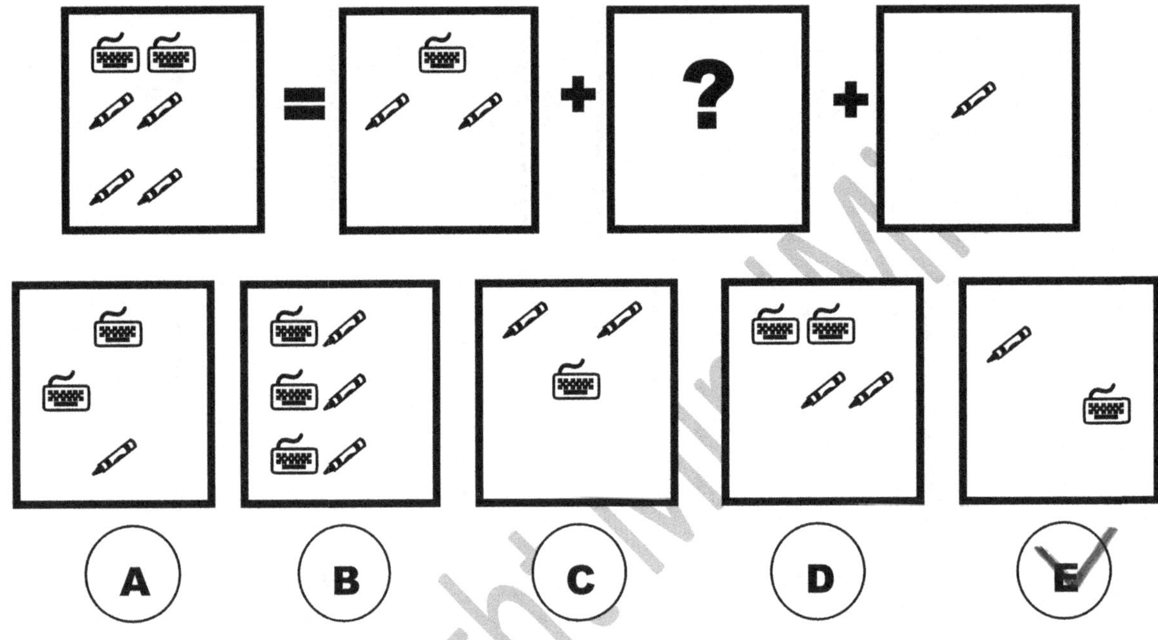

Question 12

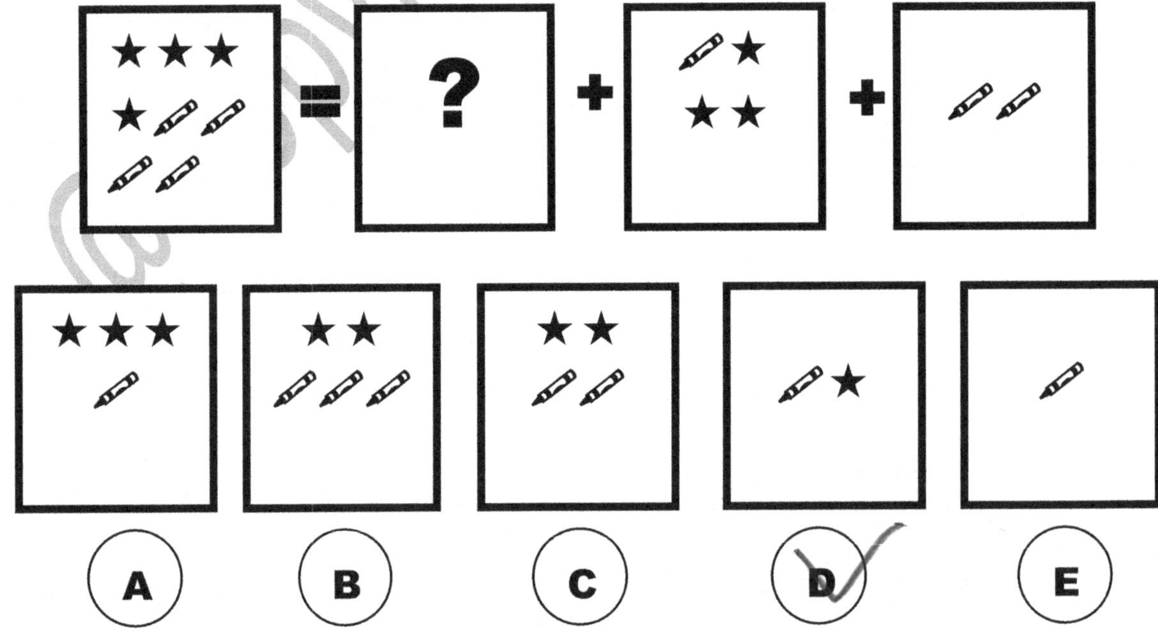

Question 13

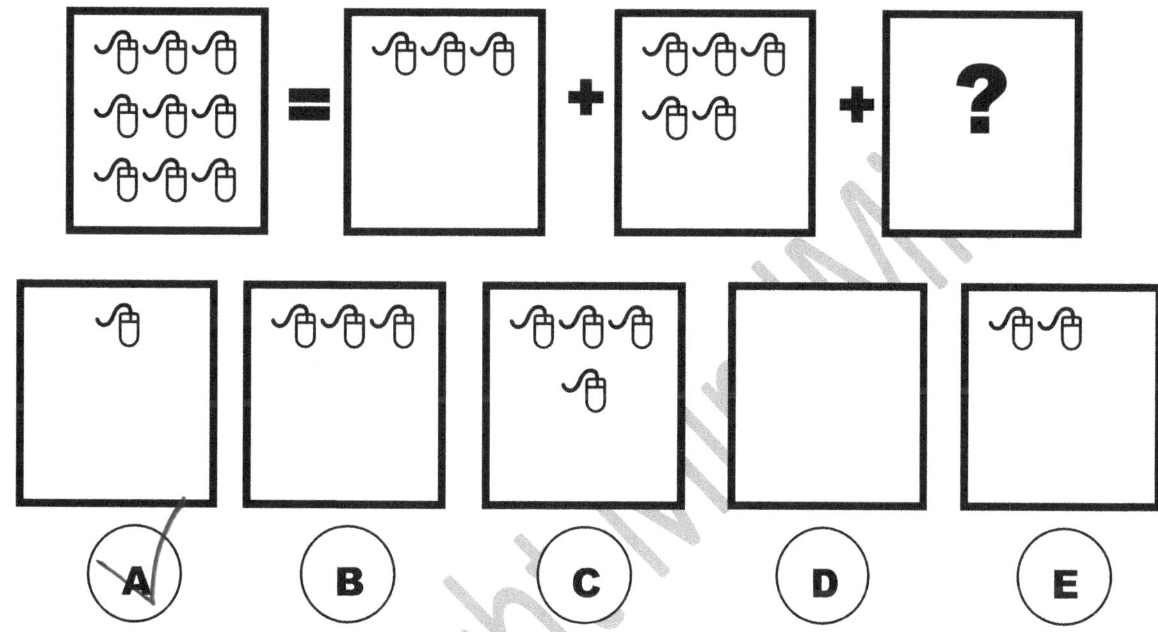

Question 14

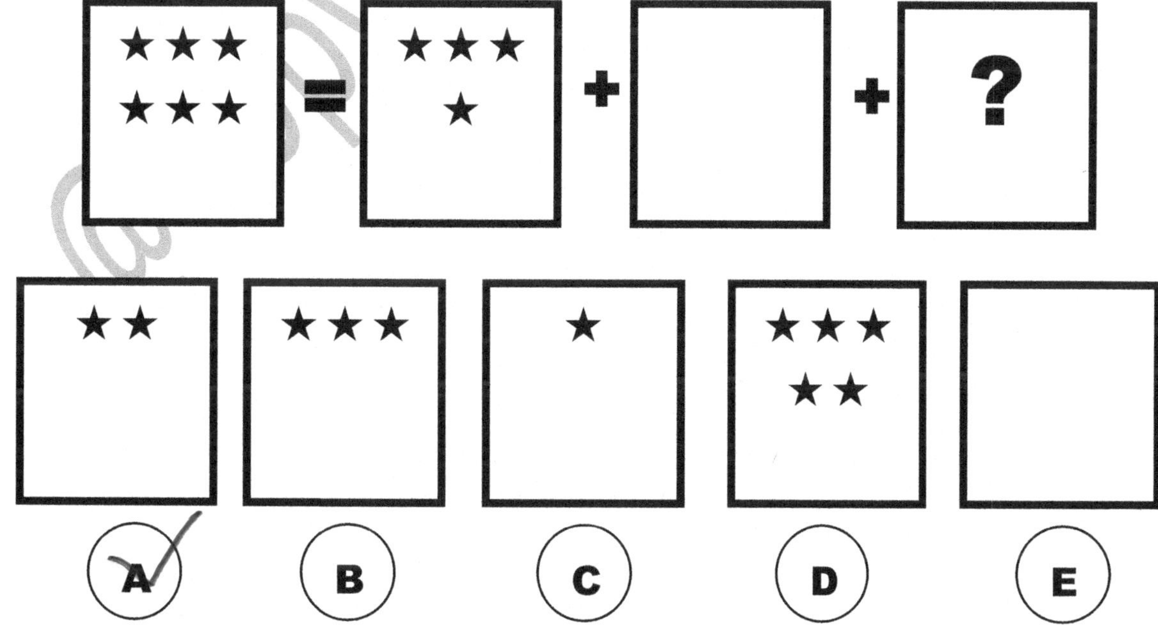

Question 15

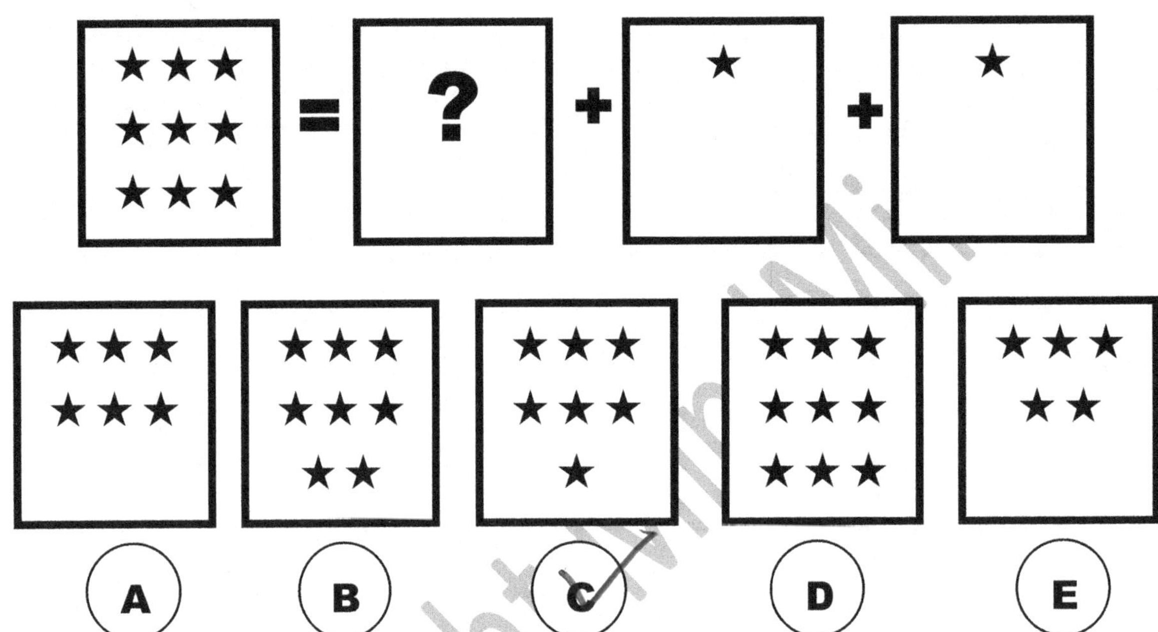

PRACTICE TEST-2

Question 1

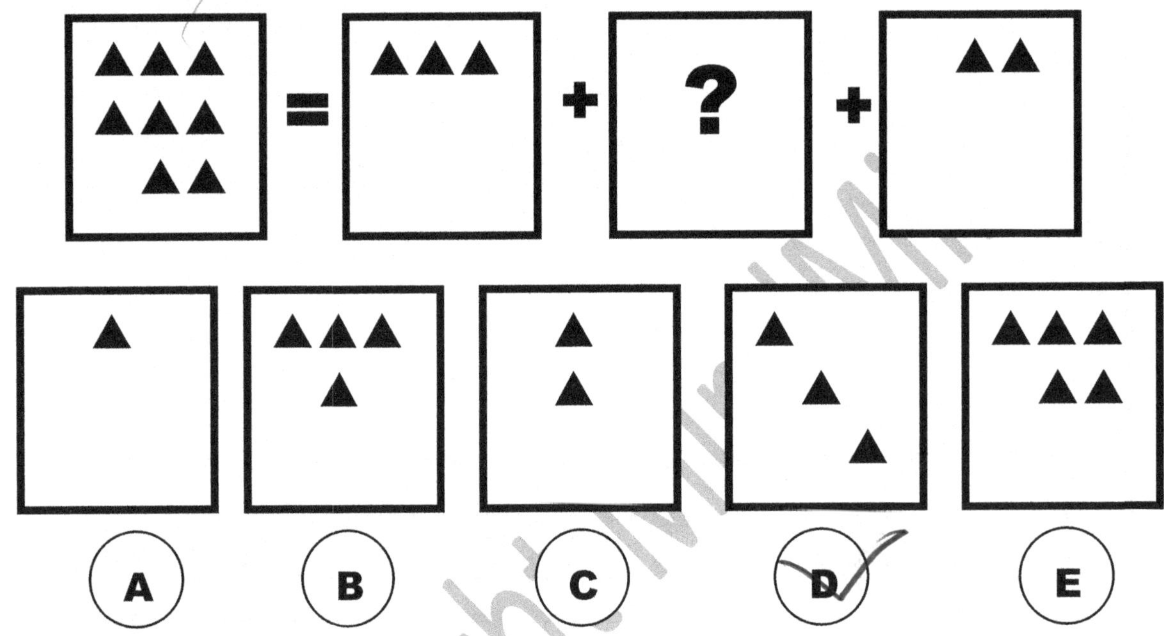

Question 2

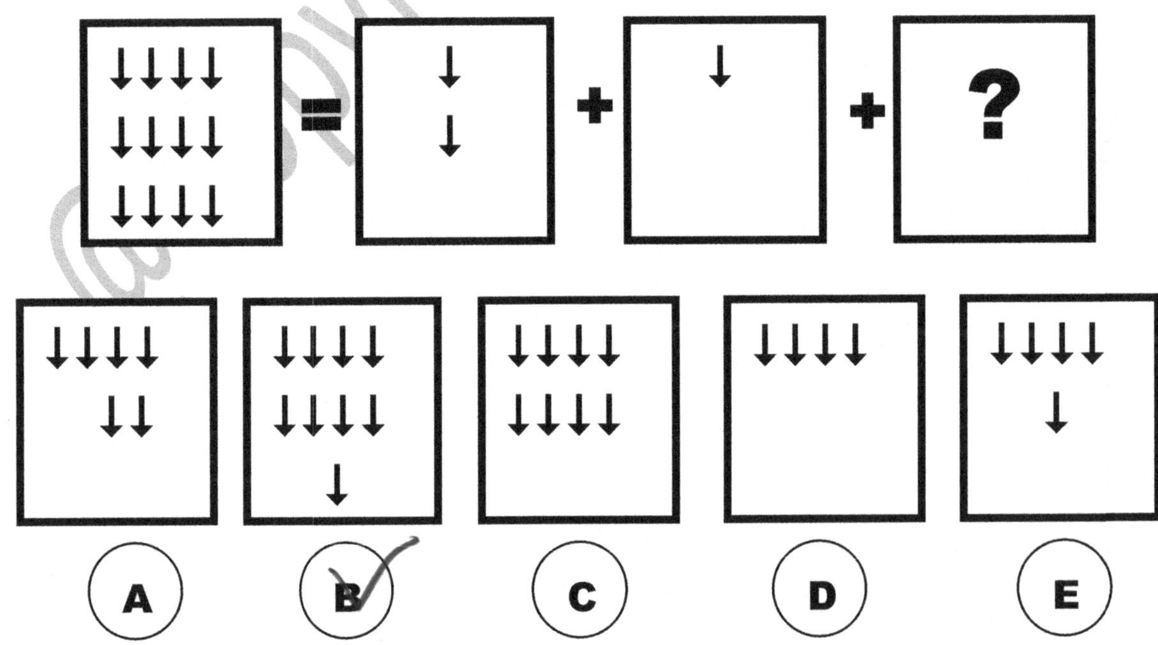

Question 3

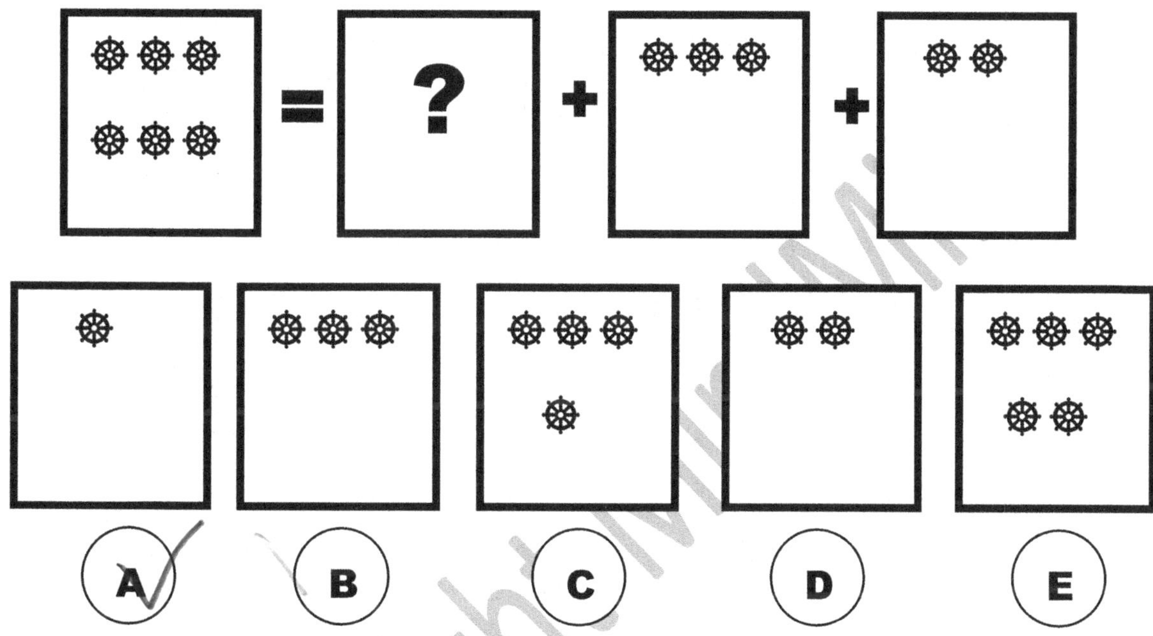

Question 4

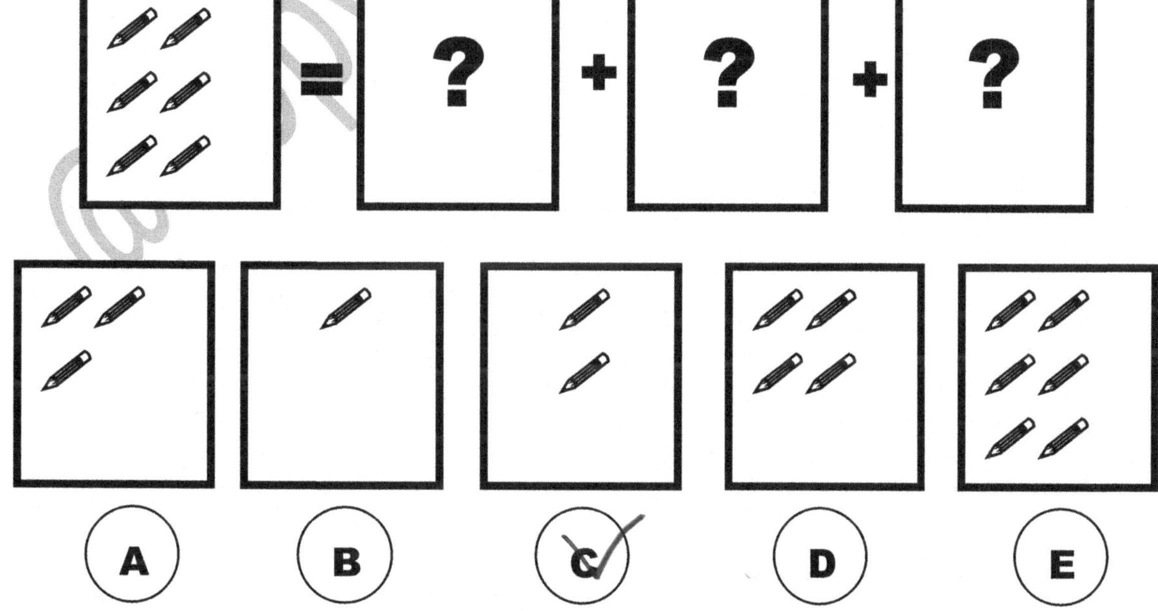

Question 5

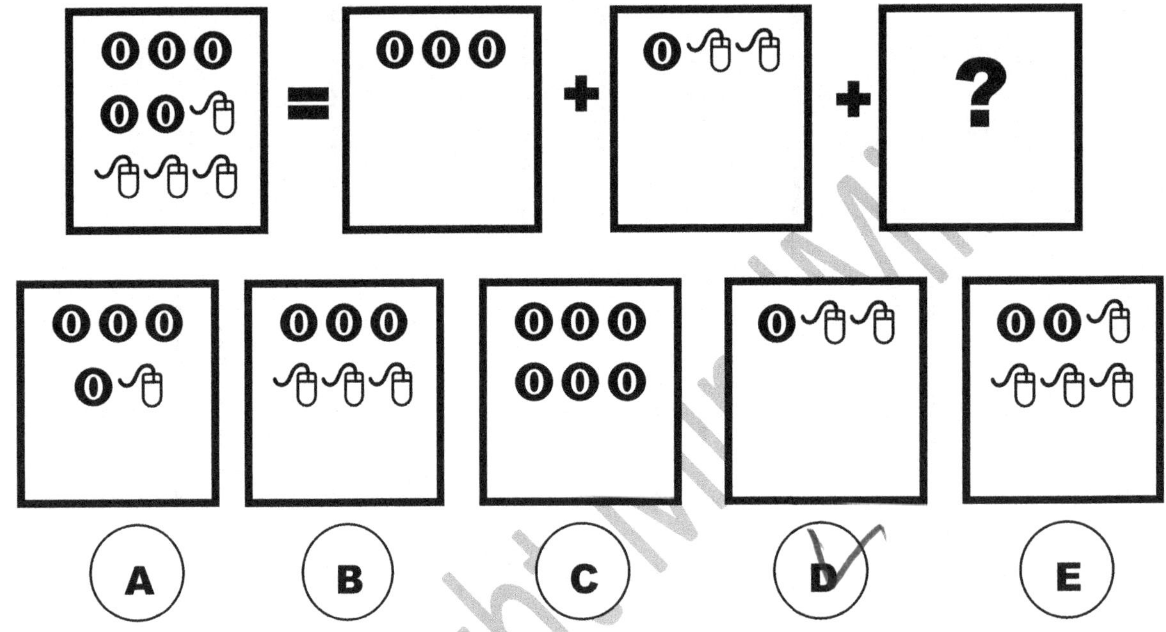

Question 6

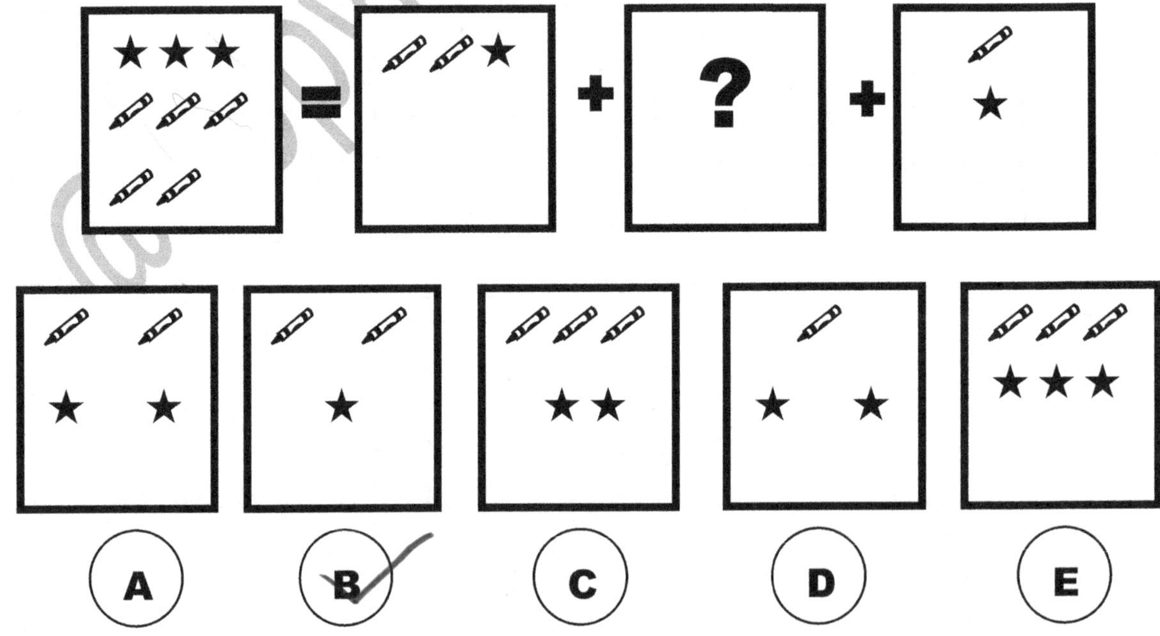

Question 7

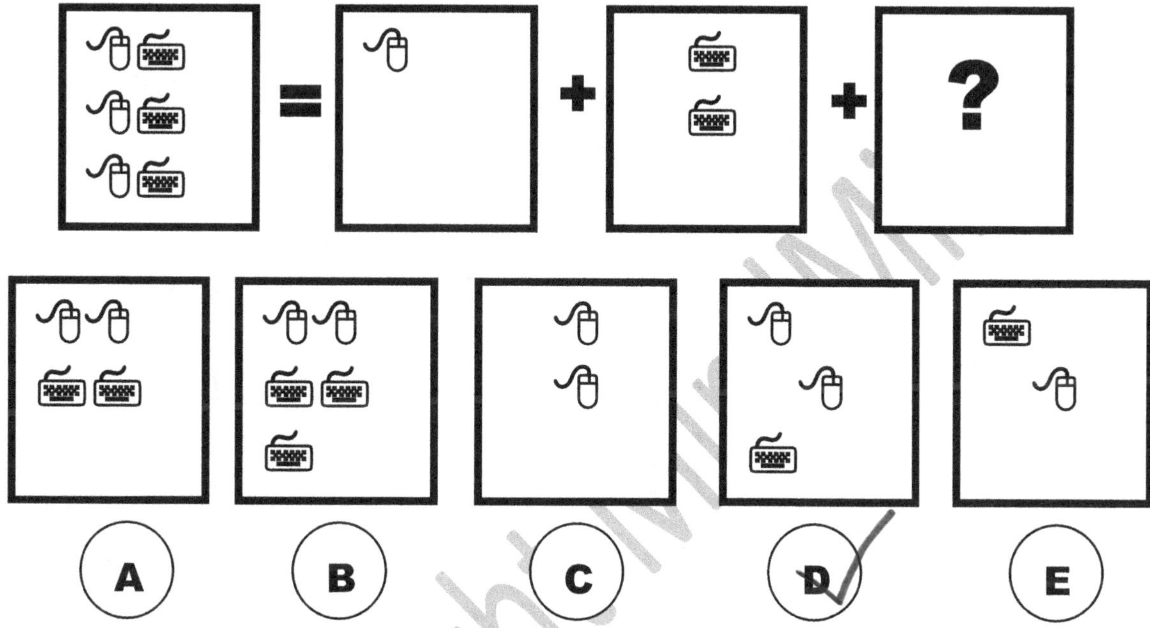

Question 8

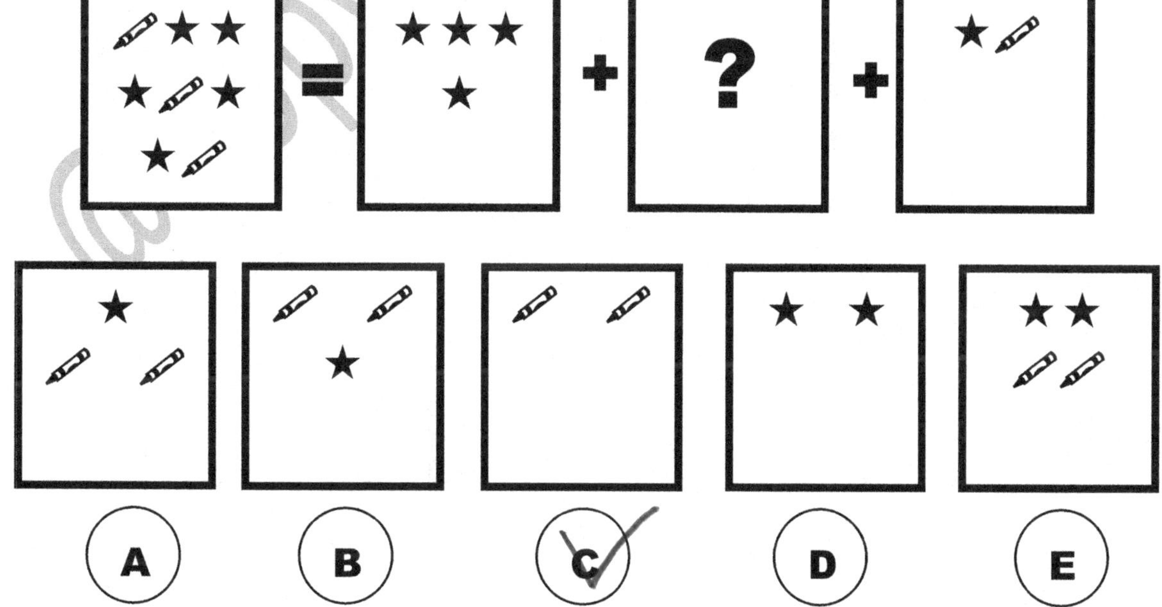

Question 9

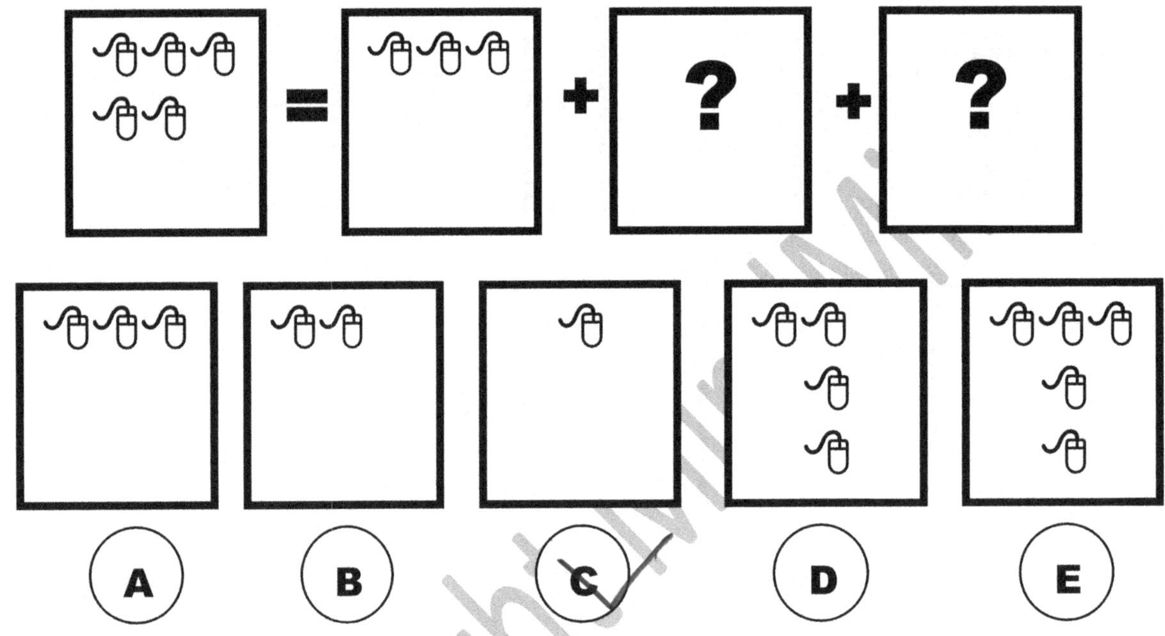

Question 10

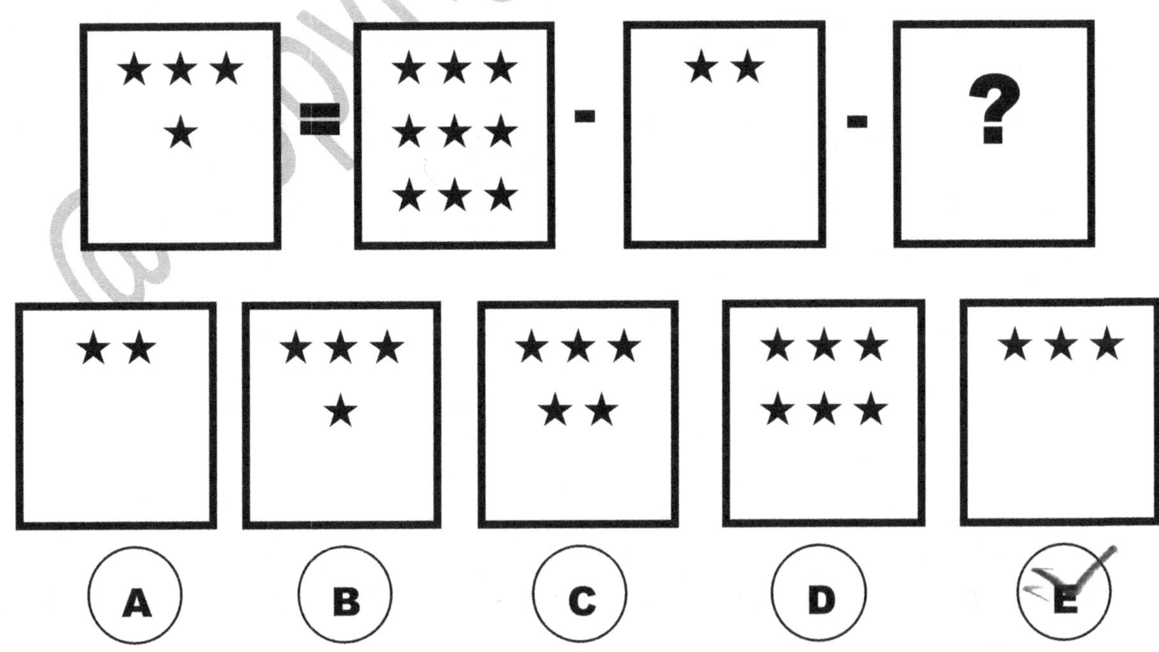

Question 11

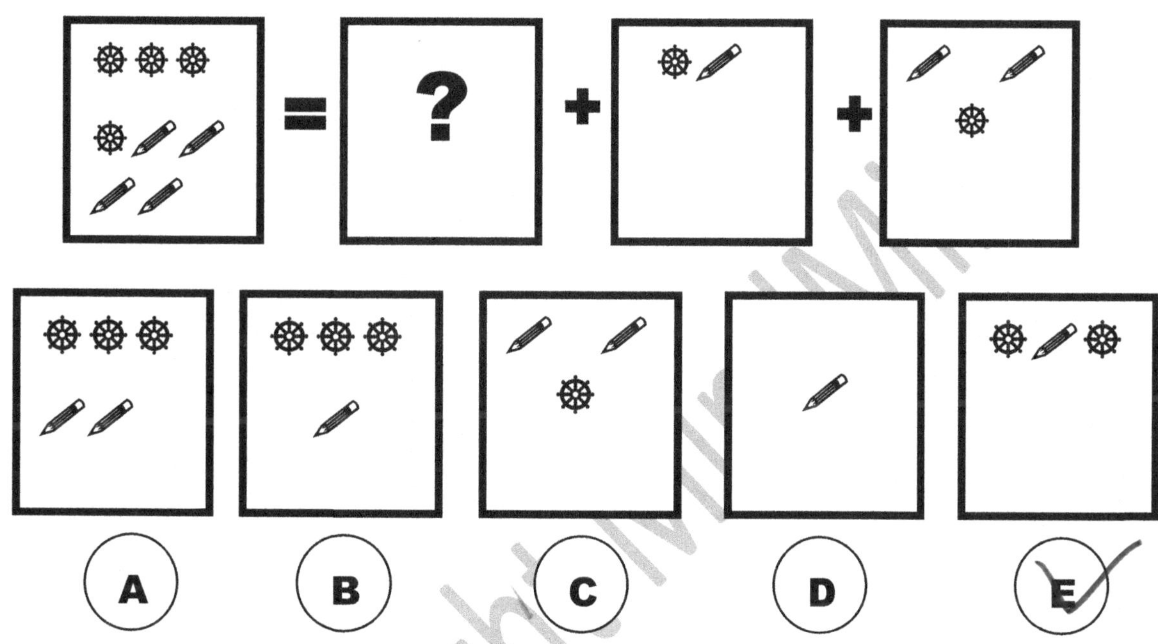

Question 12

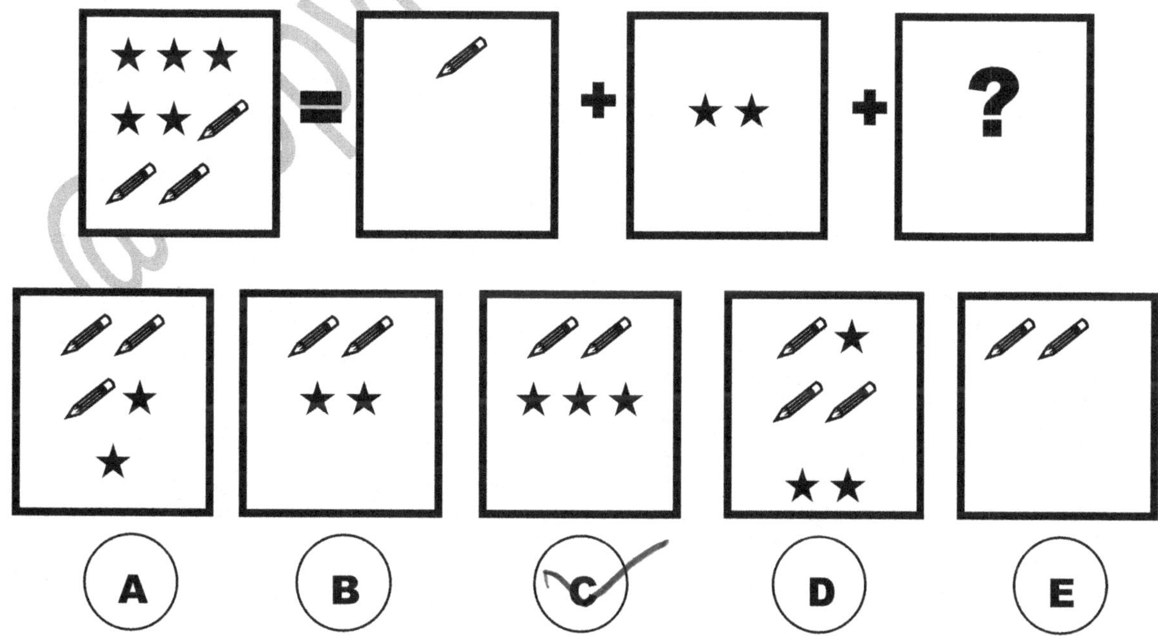

Question 13

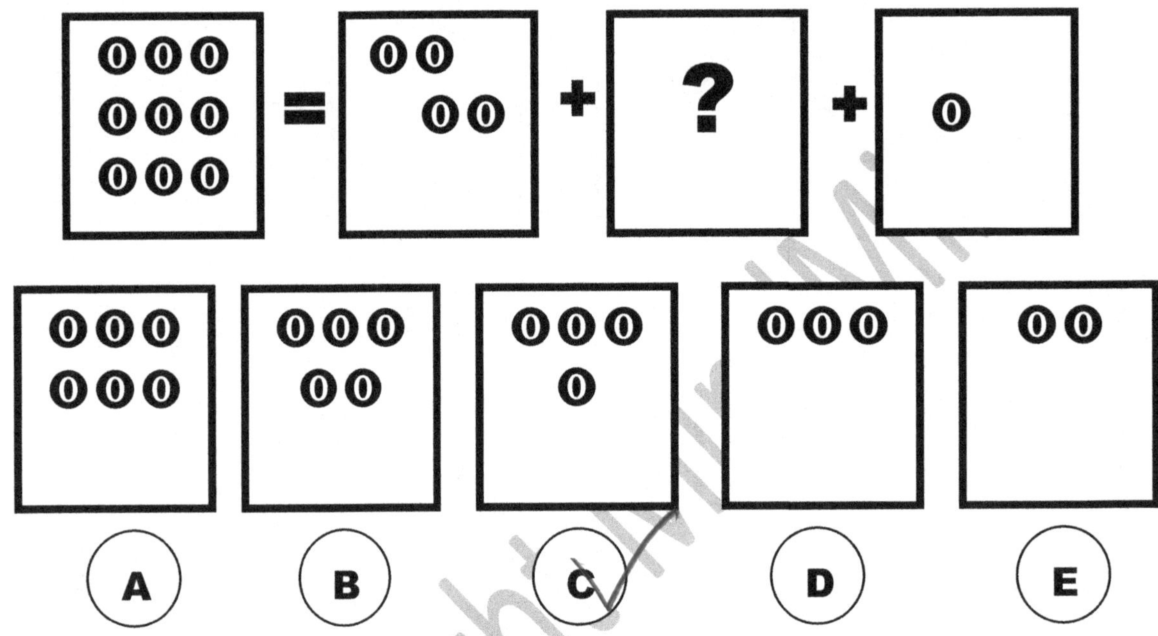

Question 14

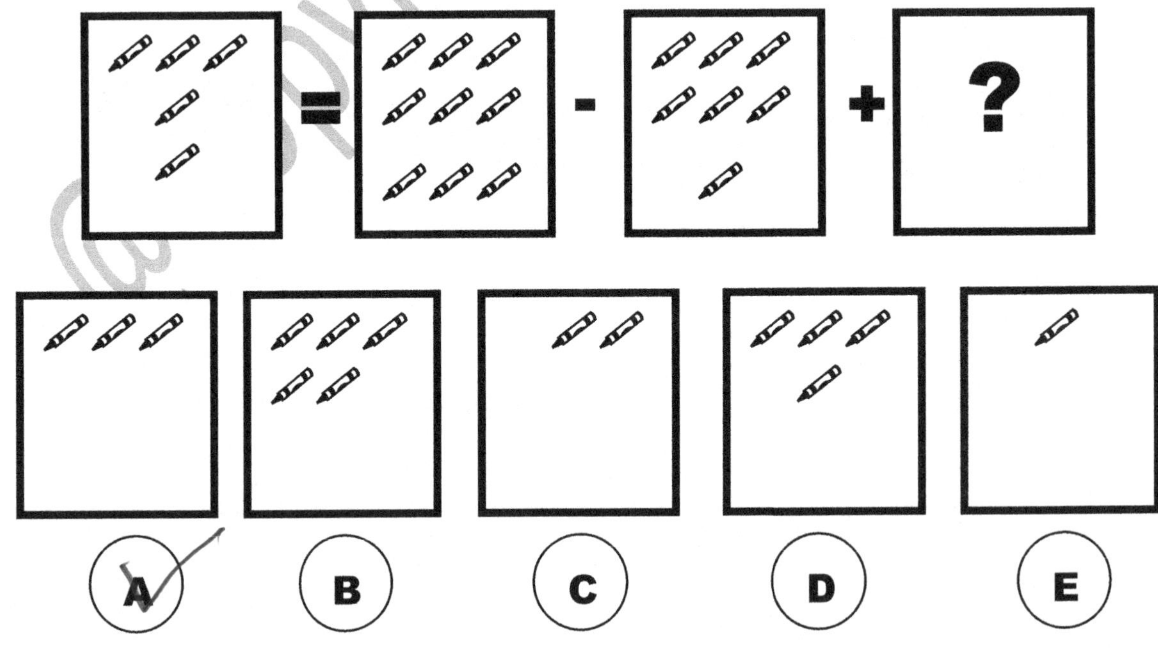

Question 15

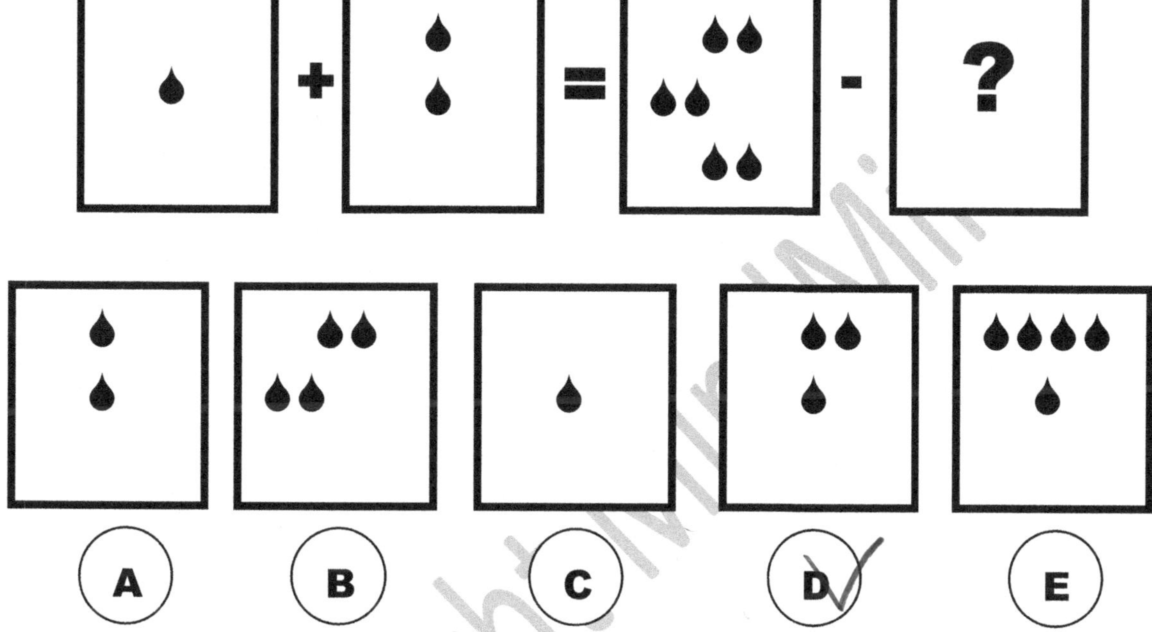

NUMBER PUZZLES

in

NUMBER FORMAT

One-Step

Two-Step

&

Multi-Step

Equations

ADDITION

Question 1

9 = 5 + ?

3	4	5	1	9
A	B	C	D	E

Question 2

7 = 4 + ?

4	5	3	1	6
A	B	C	D	E

Question 3

6 = ? + 6

1	0	6	5	2
A	B	C	D	E

Question 4

8 = 2 + ?

6	4	5	1	3
A	B	C	D	E

Question 5

3 = 1 + ?

0	5	3	1	2
A	B	C	D	E

Question 6

5 = ? + 2

1	0	3	5	2
A	B	C	D	E

Question 7

2	=	1	+	?

3 (A) 4 (B) 5 (C) 1 (D) 0 (E)

Question 8

10	=	4	+	?

4 (A) 5 (B) 3 (C) 1 (D) 6 (E)

Question 9

11	=	?	+	7

4 (A) 9 (B) 6 (C) 5 (D) 2 (E)

Question 10

15	=	5	+	?

5	10	8	7	9
A	B	C	D	E

Question 11

12	=	8	+	?

4	5	3	1	6
A	B	C	D	E

Question 12

6	=	?	+	3

1	0	3	5	2
A	B	C	D	E

Question 13

2 + 8 = 5 + ?

5	10	8	7	9
A	B	C	D	E

Question 14

7 + 5 = 8 + ?

4	5	3	1	6
A	B	C	D	E

Question 15

11 + 3 = ? + 8

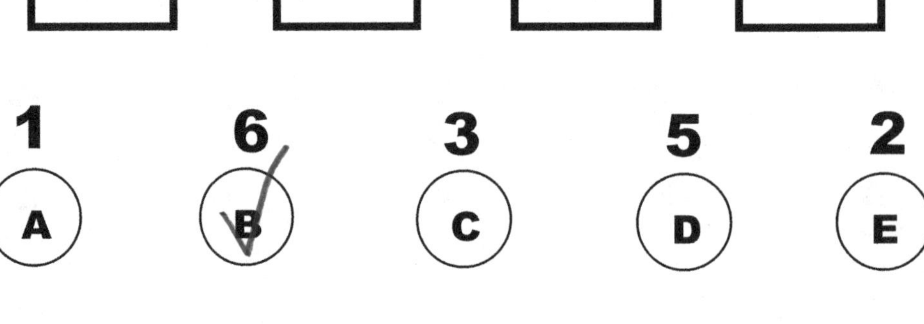

1	6	3	5	2
A	B	C	D	E

Question 16

3 + 1 = ? + [ ]

0	4	8	3	9
A	B	C	D	E

Question 17

5 + 6 = 6 + ?

3	5	4	1	6
A	B	C	D	E

Question 18

3 + 4 = ? + 5

1	4	3	5	2
A	B	C	D	E

Question 19

7	+	8	=	6	+	?

A	B	C	D	E
7	4	8	3	9

Question 20

4	+	6	=	1	+	?

A	B	C	D	E
3	9	4	8	6

Question 21

7	+	7	=	?	+	9

A	B	C	D	E
1	4	3	5	2

Question 22

1 + 5 = 6 + ?

A	B	C	D	E
1	4	0	6	9

Question 23

8 + 7 = 9 + ?

A	B	C	D	E
3	9	4	8	6

Question 24

9 + 9 = ? + 9

A	B	C	D	E
6	9	8	7	2

Question 25

8 + 4 = 6 + 3 + ?

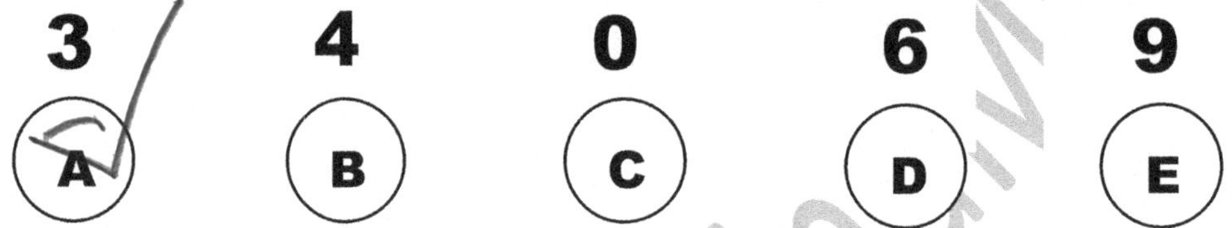

Question 26

5 + 3 = 2 + ? + 2

3 (A) 9 (B) 4 (C) 8 (D) 6 (E)

Question 27

6 + 9 = ? + 9 + 3

5 (A) 9 (B) 8 (C) 7 (D) 3 (E)

Question 28

8 + 5 = 3 + 1 + ?

3	7	9	8	5
A	B	C	D	E

Question 29

3 + 5 = 8 + ? +

3	1	5	4	0
A	B	C	D	E

Question 30

9 + 9 = ? + 6 + 7

5	9	6	7	3
A	B	C	D	E

Question 31

7 + 3 = 1 + 1 + ?

8	7	6	4	5
A	B	C	D	E

Question 32

2 + 6 = 4 + ? + 3

3	1	5	4	0
A	B	C	D	E

Question 33

9 + 2 = ? + 8 + 1

5	4	2	6	3
A	B	C	D	E

Question 34

1 + 8 = 2 + 5 + ?

3	0	2	4	5
A	B	C	D	E

Question 35

3 + 7 = 1 + ? + 2

3	5	7	4	6
A	B	C	D	E

Question 36

9 + 7 = ? + 8 + 7

1	4	2	5	3
A	B	C	D	E

Question 37

2 + 3 + 4 = 2 + 1 + ?

3	6	2	4	5
A	B	C	D	E

Question 38

5 + 3 + 4 = 6 + ? + 2

3	5	7	4	6
A	B	C	D	E

Question 39

6 + 5 + 7 = ? + 10 + 7

1	4	2	5	3
A	B	C	D	E

Question 40

1 + 8 + 2 = 9 + 1 + ?

A	B	C	D	E
3	6	2	4	1

Question 41

7 + 3 + 1 = 3 + ? + 5

A	B	C	D	E
3	1	2	4	6

Question 42

5 + 5 + 5 = ? + 10 +

A	B	C	D	E
1	4	2	5	3

Question 43

6 + 6 + 1 = 5 + 5 + ?

A	B	C	D	E
3	6	2	4	5

Question 44

1 + 9 + 3 = 11 + ? + 2

A	B	C	D	E
0	1	2	3	4

Question 45

2 + 4 + 6 = ? + 8 + 1

A	B	C	D	E
1	4	2	5	3

Question 46

1 + 3 + 2 = 2 + 1 + ?

3	1	2	0	5
A	B	C	D	E

Question 47

7 + 7 + 7 = 6 + ? + 8

3	5	7	4	6
A	B	C	D	E

Question 48

3 + 7 + ☐ = ? + 10 + ☐

1	0	2	4	3
A	B	C	D	E

Question 46

1	+	3	+	2	=	2	+	1	+	?

3	1	2	0	5
A	B	C	D	E

Question 47

7	+	7	+	7	=	6	+	?	+	8

3	5	7	4	6
A	B	C	D	E

Question 48

3	+	7	+		=	?	+	10	+	

1	0	2	4	3
A	B	C	D	E

Question 49

7	+	?	+	2	=	8	+	1	+	5

3	1	2	0	5
A	B	C	D	E

Question 50

?	+	4	+	6	=	6	+		+	9

3	5	7	4	6
A	B	C	D	E

One-Step
Two-Step
&
Multi-Step
Equations

SUBTRACTION

Question 1

5	=	8	-	?

3	4	5	1	0
A	B	C	D	E

Question 2

8	=	12	-	?

4	5	3	1	6
A	B	C	D	E

Question 3

3	=	7	-	?

1	0	4	5	2
A	B	C	D	E

Question 4

8	=	14	-	?

6	4	5	1	3
A	B	C	D	E

Question 5

1	=	9	-	?

0	8	5	7	6
A	B	C	D	E

Question 6

5	=	?	-	2

6	0	4	7	2
A	B	C	D	E

Question 7

2	=	6	-	?

3	4	5	1	0
A	B	C	D	E

Question 8

1	=	4	-	?

4	5	3	1	6
A	B	C	D	E

Question 9

2	=	?	-	7

4	9	6	5	2
A	B	C	D	E

Question 10

10	=	15	-	?

5	10	8	7	9
A	B	C	D	E

Question 11

9	=	11	-	?

4	5	3	1	2
A	B	C	D	E

Question 12

6	=	?	-	3

1	7	9	5	8
A	B	C	D	E

Question 13

2	+	4	=	12	-	?

5	6	8	7	9
A	B	C	D	E

Question 14

3	+	5	=	9	-	?

4	5	3	1	6
A	B	C	D	E

Question 15

1	+	3	=	?	-	3

1	6	3	5	7
A	B	C	D	E

Question 16

3	+	1	=	?	-	

0	4	8	3	9
A	B	C	D	E

Question 17

5	+	2	=	10	-	?

3	5	4	1	6
A	B	C	D	E

Question 18

3	+	4	=	?	-	1

8	9	7	5	2
A	B	C	D	E

Question 19

8	-	7	=	6	-	?

7	4	8	5	9
A	B	C	D ✓	E

Question 20

7	-	2	=	8	-	?

3	9	4	8	6
A ✓	B	C	D	E

Question 21

9	-	7	=	?	-	1

1	4	3	5	2
A	B	C ✓	D	E

Question 22

5	-	1	=	8	-	?

1	4	0	6	9
A	B	C	D	E

Question 23

8	-	5	=	9	-	?

3	9	4	8	6
A	B	C	D	E

Question 24

9	-	9	=	?	-	9

6	9	8	7	2
A	B	C	D	E

Question 25

4	+	2	=	9	-	1	-	?

A	B	C	D	E
3	4	0	6	2

Question 26

5	+	3	=	10	+	?	-	2

A	B	C	D	E
3	0	4	1	6

Question 27

2	+	5	=	?	+	9	-	3

A	B	C	D	E
5	2	1	4	3

Question 28

4	+	1	=	11	+	1	-	?

3	7	9	8	5
A	B ✓	C	D	E

Question 29

2	+	2	=	8	-	?	-	

3	1	5	4	0
A	B	C	D ✓	E

Question 30

5	+	1	=	?	-	1	-	1

8	9	6	7	3
A ✓	B	C	D	E

Question 31

7 - 3 = 10 - 5 - ?

1	2	3	4	5
A ✓	B	C	D	E

Question 32

9 - 6 = 8 - ? - 3

3	1	5	4	2
A	B	C	D	E ✓

Question 33

8 - 2 = ? - 2 - 1

5	9	2	6	8
A	B ✓	C	D	E

Question 34

1 + 1 = 8 + 1 - ?

3 (A) 6 (B) 7 (C) 4 (D) 5 (E)

Question 35

3 + 8 = 9 + ? - 2

3 (A) 5 (B) 7 (C) 4 (D) 6 (E)

Question 36

2 + 5 = ? + 1 - 1

7 (A) 4 (B) 2 (C) 6 (D) 9 (E)

Question 37

2	+	3	-	4	=	5	-	1	-	?

3	6	2	4	5
A	B	C	D	E

Question 38

5	+	3	-	4	=	6	-	?	-	2

3	2	1	4	0
A	B	C	D	E

Question 39

6	-	5	+	1	=	?	-	1	+	1

1	4	2	5	3
A	B	C	D	E

Question 40

1	+	8	-	2	=	9	-	5	+	?

3	6	2	4	1
A	B	C	D	E

Question 41

7	+	2	-	9	=	3	-	?	-	1

3	1	2	4	6
A	B	C	D	E

Question 42

5	+	5	-	5	=	?	+	4	-	3

1	4	2	5	3
A	B	C	D	E

Question 43

6	-	6	+	1	=	5	+	5	-	?

A	B	C	D	E
3	6	2	9	7

Question 44

9	-	5	+	3	=	11	+	?	-	6

A	B	C	D	E
0	1	2	3	4

Question 45

7	-	4	+	2	=	?	+	8	-	3

A	B	C	D	E
1	4	2	5	0

Question 46

7 - 6 + 1 = 2 + 1 - ?

3	1	2	0	5
A	B	C	D	E

Question 47

7 - 5 + [ ] = 9 + ? - 8

3	5	1	4	2
A	B	C	D	E

Question 48

9 - 8 + 1 = ? + 10 - 8

1	0	2	4	3
A	B	C	D	E

Question 49

7	-	?	+	2	=	8	-	3	+	2

3	1	2	0	5
A	B	C ✓	D	E

Question 50

?	-	4	+	6	=	6	-		+	3

3	5	7	4	6
A	B	C ✓	D	E

One-Step Two-Step & Multi-Step Equations

DIVISION

Question 1

8 = ? + ?

3	4	5	1	9
A	B	C	D	E

Question 2

6 = ? + ?

4	5	3	1	6
A	B	C	D	E

Question 3

4 = ? + ?

1	0	6	5	2
A	B	C	D	E

Question 4

2 = **?** + **?**

A	B	C	D	E
6	4	5	1	3

Question 5

10 = **?** + **?**

A	B	C	D	E
0	5	3	1	2

Question 6

12 = **?** + **?**

A	B	C	D	E
1	4	6	5	2

Question 7

$$20 = ? + ?$$

3	10	8	11	0
A	B	C	D	E

Question 8

$$14 = ? + ?$$

4	5	7	9	6
A	B	C	D	E

Question 9

$$16 = ? + ?$$

4	9	6	8	7
A	B	C	D	E

Question 10

2	=	?	+	?

5	1	3	2	9
A	B	C	D	E

Question 11

12	=	?	+	?

4	5	3	1	6
A	B	C	D	E

Question 12

10	=	?	+	?

1	0	3	5	2
A	B	C	D	E

Question 13

2 + 6 = ? + ?

5	8	3	7	4
A	B	C	D	E ✓

Question 14

7 + 5 = ? + ?

4	5	3	1	6
A	B	C	D	E ✓

Question 15

11 + 3 = ? + ?

1	6	7	5	2
A	B	C ✓	D	E

Question 16

3 + 1 = ? + ?

0	4	2	3	6
A	B	C	D	E

Question 17

4 + 6 = ? + ?

3	5	4	1	6
A	B	C	D	E

Question 18

8 + 4 = ? + ?

1	4	6	5	8
A	B	C	D	E

Question 19

7	+	5	=	6	+	?	+	?

7 (A) 4 (B) 8 (C) 3 (D) 9 (E)

Question 20

4	+	5	=	1	+	?	+	?

3 (A) 9 (B) 4 (C) 8 (D) 6 (E)

Question 21

7	+	9	=	?	+	6	+	?

1 (A) 4 (B) 3 (C) 5 (D) 2 (E)

Question 22

1	+	5	=	6	+	?	+	?

1	4	0	6	9
A	B	C	D	E

Question 23

3	+	8	=	?	+	3	+	?

3	9	5	8	4
A	B	C	D	E

Question 24

10	+	9	=	?	+	9	+	?

6	5	8	7	9
A	B	C	D	E

Question 25

8 + 4 = ? + ? + ?

3	4	5	6	9
A	B	C	D	E

Question 26

5 + 4 = ? + ? + ?

3	9	4	8	6
A	B	C	D	E

Question 27

6 + 9 = ? + ? + ?

5	9	8	7	3
A	B	C	D	E

Question 28

9 + 9 = ? + ? + ?

3	7	8	6	5
A	B	C	D	E

Question 29

2 + 1 = ? + ? + ?

3	1	5	4	0
A	B	C	D	E

Question 30

1 + 5 = ? + ? + ?

5	2	6	7	3
A	B	C	D	E

Question 31

7	+	3	=	?	+	2	+	?

8	7	6	4	5
A	B	C	D	E

Question 32

2	+	6	=	?	+	?	+	4

3	8	5	4	2
A	B	C	D	E

Question 33

9	+	3	=	?	+	?	+	4

5	4	8	6	3
A	B	C	D	E

Question 34

5	+	9	=	?	+	8	+	?

3	6	2	4	5
A	B	C	D	E

Question 35

3	+	5	=	6	+	?	+	?

2	5	1	4	8
A	B	C	D	E

Question 36

9	+	7	=	?	+	?	+	8

1	4	2	5	8
A	B	C	D	E

Question 37

2	+	9	+	4	=	?	+	5	+	?

A	B	C	D	E
3	6	2	4	5

Question 38

5	+	4	+	4	=	?	+	?	+	5

A	B	C	D	E
8	5	7	4	6

Question 39

4	+	5	+	6	=	?	+	9	+	?

A	B	C	D	E
6	4	2	5	3

Question 40

3	+	8	+	7	=	8	+	?	+	?

9	6	5	4	10
A	B	C	D	E

Question 41

1	+	3	+	2	=	?	+	?	+	4

3	1	2	4	6
A	B	C	D	E

Question 42

5	+	8	+	7	=	?	+	?	+	8

8	4	6	5	9
A	B	C	D	E

Question 43

6	+	6	+	8	=	?	+	12	+	?

3	6	2	4	8
A	B	C	D	E

Question 44

1	+	9	+	3	=	7	+	?	+	?

0	6	2	3	4
A	B	C	D	E

Question 45

5	+	4	+	6	=	?	+	?	+	9

1	4	6	5	3
A	B	C	D	E

Question 46

1	+	7	+	5	=	?	+	9	+	?

A	B	C	D	E
3	1	2	4	5

Question 47

7	+	7	+	7	=	?	+	?	+	11

A	B	C	D	E
3	5	7	4	6

Question 48

	+	7	+		=	?	+	?	+	1

A	B	C	D	E
1	0	2	4	3

Question 49

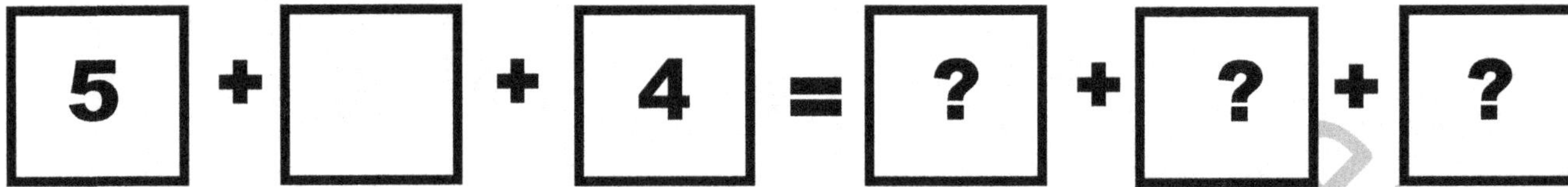

3	1	2	9	5
A	B	C	D	E

Question 50

3	5	7	9	6
A	B	C	D	E

ANSWERS

1: If you see SAME Number with Same Sign on both sides of Equal sign (=), Simply strike out (Eliminate from equation)

5 + ~~2~~ = 3 + ~~2~~ + ?

2: Use Number Facts

9 + 3 = 7 + ?

~~7~~ + 2 + 3 = ~~7~~ + ?

2 + 3 = ?

(Number Fact: 9 = 7 + 2)

3: Use "Adding Doubles"

1 + 9 + 3 = 7 + ? + ?

1 + ~~7~~ + 2 + 3 = ~~7~~ + ? + ?

6 = ? + ?

6 = 3 + 3 (Adding Doubles)

TIPS

NUMBER PUZZLES

in

PICTURE FORMAT

One-Step Equations

ADDITION

QUESTION		ANSWER
1	9 = 6 + ? 9 = 6 + **3**	C
2	6 = ? + 4 6 = **2** + 4	C
3	9 = 1 + ? 9 = 1 + **8**	A
4	8 = 5 + ? 8 = 5 + **3**	E
5	9 = ? + 0 9 = **9** + 0	E
6	15 = 10 + ? 15 = 10 + **5**	D
7	8 = ? + 2 8 = **6** + 2	A
8	15 = 11 + ? 15 = 11+ **4**	B
9	9 = 2 + ? 9 = 2 + **7**	B
10	3 = 1 + ? 3 = 1 + **2**	A

One-Step Equations

SUBTRACTION

QUESTION		ANSWER
1	4 = 9 - ? 4 = 9 - **5**	B
2	4 = ? - 4 4 = **8** - 4	C
3	3 = 9 - ? 3 = 9 – **6**	C
4	1 = 8 - ? 1 = 8 – **7**	E
5	9 = ? – 0 9 = **9** - 0	E
6	1 = 10 - ? 1 = 10 – **9**	E
7	3 = ? - 2 3 = **5** - 2	D
8	8 = 11 - ? 8 = 11- **3**	C
9	2 = 8 - ? 2 = 8 – **6**	C
10	3 = 3 - ? 3 = 3 - **0**	C

One-Step Equations

DIVISION

QUESTION		ANSWER
1	8 = ? + ? 8 = **4** + **4**	E
2	6 = ? + ? 6 = **3** + **3**	A
3	6 = ? + ? 6 = **3** + **3**	B
4	4 = ? + ? 4 = **2** + **2**	A
5	2 = ? + ? 2 = **1** + **1**	C
6	12 = ? + ? 12 = **6** + **6**	B
7	4 = ? + ? 4 = **2** + **2**	D
8	10 = ? + ? 10 = **5**+ **5**	E
9	8 = ? + ? 8 = **4** + **4**	B
10	2 = ? + ? 2 = **1** + **1**	B

Two-Step Equations

Addition & Addition

QUESTION		ANSWER
1	1 + 3 = 2 + ? 4 = 2 + **?** 4 = 2 + **2**	C
2	5 + 2 = 4 + ? 7 = 4 + **?** 7 = 4 + **3**	A
3	4 + 6 = 9 + ? 10 = 9 + **?** 10 = 9 + **1**	C
4	6 + 2 = 3 + ? 8 = 3 + **?** 8 = 3 + **5**	E
5	4 + 5 = 6 + ? 9 = 6 + **?** 9 = 6 + **3**	E
6	9 + ~~9~~ = ~~9~~ + ? 9 = 0 + **?** 9 = 0 + **9**	A
7	12 + 8 = 10 + ? 20 = 10 + **?** 20 = 10 + **10**	A

8	9 + ~~6~~ = ? + ~~6~~ 9 = **?** + 0 9 = **9** + 0	E
9	? + 6 = 5 + 5 **?** + 6 = 10 **4** + 6 = 10	C
10	2 + 4 = 5 + ? 6 = 5 + **?** 6 = 5 + **1**	D

Two-Step Equations

Addition & Subtraction

QUESTION		ANSWER
1	3 + 2 = 6 - ? 5 = 6 - **?** 5 = 6 – **1**	**C**
2	1 + 2 = 6 - ? 3 = 6 - **?** 3 = 6 - **3**	**E**
3	8 + 3 = 12 - ? 11 = 12 - **?** 11 = 12 - **1**	**C**
4	1 + 0 = 9 - ? 1 = 9 - **?** 1 = 9 – **8**	**D**
5	0 + ~~6~~ = ~~6~~ - ? 0 = **?** 0 = **0**	**B**
6	5 + 2 = 9 - ? 7 = 9 - **?** 7 = 9 – **2**	**A**
7	1 + 1 = 12 - ? 2 = 12 - **?** 2 = 12 - **10**	**D**

8	2 + **?** = 8 - 1 2 + **?** = 7 2 + **5** = 7	**D**
9	? + 2 = 6 - 1 **?** + 2 = 5 **3** + 2 = 5	**C**
10	1 + ? = 2 - 0 1 + **?** = 2 1 + **1** = 2	**A**

Two-Step Equations

Addition & Division

QUESTION		ANSWER
1	12 + 8 = ? + ? 20 = ? + ? 20 = **10** + **10**	**B**
2	6 + 2 = ? + ? 8 = ? + ? 8 = **4** + **4**	**B**
3	10 + 8 = ? + ? 18 = ? + ? 18 = **9** + **9**	**E**
4	3 + 1 = ? + ? 4 = ? + ? 4 = **2** + **2**	**A**
5	6 + 0 = ? + ? 6 = ? + ? 6 = **3 + 3**	**C**
6	? + ? = 9 + 9 ? + ? = 18 **9** + **9** = 18	**C**
7	? + ? = 12 + 6 ? + ? = 18 **9** + **9** = 18	**B**

8	? + ? = 6 + 4 ? + ? = 10 **5** + **5** = 10	D
9	? + ? = 3 + 1 ? + ? = 4 **2** + **2** = 4	A
10	? + ? = 5 + 3 ? + ? = 8 **4** + **4** = 8	D

Multi-Step Equations Using

Addition

Subtraction

&

Division

QUESTION		ANSWER
1	6 + ~~5~~ = 4 + ~~5~~ + ? 6 = 4 + ? 6 = 4 + **2**	**D**
2	~~9~~ + ~~7~~ = ~~7~~ + ? + ~~9~~ 0 = 0 + ? 0 = **0**	**B**
3	8 + 6 = ? + 3 + 5 ~~8~~ + 6 = ? + ~~8~~ 6 = ? 6 = **6**	**A**
4	6 + ~~5~~ = 2 + ~~5~~ + ? 6 = 2 + ? 6 = 2 + **4**	**C**
5	~~4~~ + 6 = ? + ~~4~~ + 3 6 = ? + 3 6 = **3** + 3	**D**
6	8 + ~~7~~ = ~~7~~ + ? + 3 8 = ? + 3 8 = **5** + 3	**E**

7	10 + 5 = ? + 1 + 4 10 + ~~5~~ = ? + ~~5~~ 10 = ? 10 = **10**	**A**
8	6 + 5 = 7 + 3 + ? 11 = 10 + ? 11 = 10 + **1**	**B**
9	6 + 3 = 5 + ? + 1 ~~6~~ + 3 = ~~6~~ + ? 3 = **?**	**E**
10	4 + 3 = ? + 1 + 1 7 = ? + 2 7 = **5** + 2	**B**
11	2 + ~~6~~ = ~~6~~ + 5 - ? 2 = 5 - ? 2 = 5 - **3**	**C**
12	5 + 2 = 9 - ? + 1 7 = 10 - ? 7 = 10 - **3**	**D**
13	~~8~~ + 6 = 12 + ~~8~~ - ? 6 = 12 - ? 6 = 12 - **6**	**D**

14	4 + ~~2~~ = 8 - ? + ~~2~~ 4 = 8 - ? 4 = 8 – **4**	**B**
15	4 + 3 = 5 + 6 - ? 7 = 11 - ? 7 = 11 – **4**	**E**
16	~~9~~ + 5 = 9 - ? + ~~9~~ 5 = 9 - ? 5 = 9 – **4**	**B**
17	8 + ~~4~~ = 12 + ~~4~~ - ? 8 = 12 - ? 8 = 12 – **4**	**E**
18	~~3~~ + 2 = 7 - ? + ~~3~~ 2 = 7 - ? 2 = 7 – **5**	**A**
19	4 + 2 = 6 + 0 - ? ~~6~~ = ~~6~~ - ? 0 = ? 0 = 0	**B**
20	1 + 3 = ? - 6 + 6 4 = ? - 0 4 = **4** - 0	**B**

21	4 + 6 = 2 + ? + ? 10 = 2 + ? + ? 10 = 2 + **4 + 4**	**C**
22	9 + 5 = ? + 4 + ? 14 = ? + 4 + ? 14 = **5** + 4 + **5**	**A**
23	7 + 8 = ? + ? + ? 15 = ? + ? + ? 15 = **5** + **5** + **5**	**E**
24	? + ? = 6 + 3 + 1 ? + ? = 10 **5** + **5** = 10	**B**
25	6 + 4 = ? + ? + 2 10 = ? + ? + 2 10 = **4** + **4** + 2	**A**
26	4 + ~~5~~ = ~~5~~ + ? + ? 4 = ? + ? 4 = **2** + **2**	**B**
27	? + ? = 2 + 5 + 1 ? + ? = 8 **4** + **4** = 8	**B**

28	9 + 9 = ? + ? + ? 18 = ? + ? + ? 18 = **6** + **6** + **6**	**A**
29	6 + ~~6~~ = ? + ~~6~~ + ? 6 = ? + ? 6 = **3** + **3**	**E**
30	4 + 5 = ? + ? + 3 9 = ? + ? + 3 9 = **3** + **3** + 3	**C**

PRACTICE TEST-1

QUESTION		ANSWER
1	8 = 5 + 1 + ? 8 = 6 + ? 8 = 6 + **2**	**E**
2	5 = 2 + 1 + ? 5 = 3 + ? 5 = 3 + **2**	**A**
3	9 = 8 + 6 - ? 9 = 14 - ? 9 = 14 - **5**	**C**
4	? = 4 + 6 + 2 ? = 12 **12** = 12	**E**
5	When there are different types of pictures, consider them as separate problems 6 Triangles = 2 Triangles + ? + 1 Traingle 6 = 2 + ? + 1 6 = 3 + ? 6 = 3 + **3** **(3 Traingles)**	**C**

	2 Keyboards = ? + 0 2 = 2 2 = 2 **(2 Keyboards)** Ans: 3 Triangles & 2 Keyboards	
6	When there are different types of pictures, consider them as separate problems 7 Arrows = 1 Arrow + 1 Arrow + ? 7 = 1 + 1 + ? 7 = 2 + ? 7 = 2 + **5** **(5 Arrows)** 3 Wheels = 1 Wheel + 2 Wheels + ? 3 = 1 + 2 + ? 3 = 3 + ? 3 = 3 + **0** **(0 Wheels)** Ans: 5 Arrows & 0 Wheels	**E**

7	6 = ? + ? + 4 6 = **1** + **1** + 4	D
8	6 = ? + ? + ? 6 = **2** + **2** + **2**	C
9	6 = 1 + 3 + ? 6 = 4 + ? 6 = 4 + **2**	D
10	6 = 0 + ? + 1 6 = ? + 1 6 = **5** + 1	B
11	When there are different types of pictures, consider them as separate problems 2 Keyboards = 1 Keyboard + ? + 0 Keyboard 2 = 1 + ? + 0 2 = 1 + ? 2 = 1 + **1** **(1 Keyboard)** 4 Crayons = 2 Crayons + ? + 1 Crayon	E

	4 = 2 + ? +1 4 = 3 + ? 4 = 3 **+ 1** **(1 Crayon)** Ans: 1 Keyboard & 1 Crayon	
12	When there are different types of pictures, consider them as separate problems 4 Stars = ? + 3 stars + 0 stars 4 = ? + 3 4 = **1** + 3 **(1 Star)** 4 Crayons = ? + 1 Crayon + 2 Crayons 4 = ? + 1 + 2 4 = ? + 3 4 = **1** + 3 **(1 Crayon)** Ans: 1 Star & 1 Crayon	**D**

13	9 = 3 + 5 + ? 9 = 8 + ? 9 = 8 + **1**	**A**
14	6 = 4 + 0 + ? 6 = 4 + ? 6 = 4 + **2**	**A**
15	9 = ? + 1 + 1 9 = ? + 2 9 = 7 + **2**	**C**

PRACTICE TEST-2

QUESTION		ANSWER
1	8 = 3 + ? + 2 8 = 5 + ? 8 = 5 + **3**	**D**
2	12 = 2 + 1 + ? 12 = 3 + ? 12 = 3 + **9**	**B**
3	6 = ? + 3 + 2 6 = ? + 5 6 = **1** + 5	**A**
4	6 = ? + ? + ? 6 = **2** + **2** + **2**	**C**
5	When there are different types of pictures, consider them as separate problems 5 Circles = 3 Circles + 1 Circle + ? 5 = 3 + 1 + ? 5 = 4 + ? 5 = 4 + **1** **(1 Circle)**	**D**

	4 Mice = 0 + 2 Mice + ? 4 = 0 + 2 + ? 4 = 2 + ? 4 = 2 + **2** **(2 Mice)** Ans: 1 Circle & 2 Mice	
6	3 Stars = 1 Star + ? + 1 Star 3 = 1 + ? + 1 3 = 2 + ? 3 = 2 + **1** **(1 Star)** 5 Crayons = 2 Crayons + ? + 1 Crayon 5 = 2 + ? + 1 5 = 3 + ? 5 = 3 + **2** **(2 Crayons)** Ans: 1 Star & 2 Crayons	**B**

7	3 Mice = 1 Mice + 0 + ? 3 = 1 + 0 + ? 3 = 1 + ? 3 = 1 + **2** **(2 Mice)** 3 Keyboards = 0 + 2 Keyboards + ? 3 = 0 + 2 + ? 3 = 2 + ? 3 = 2 + **1** **(1 Keyboard)** Ans: 2 Mice & 1 Keyboard	**D**
8	3 Crayons = 0 + ? + 1 Crayon 3 = 0 + ? + 1 3 = 1 + ? 3 = 1 + **2** **(2 Crayons)** 5 Stars = 4 Stars + ? + 1 Star 5 = 4 + ? + 1	**C**

	5 = 5 + ? 5 = 5 + **0** **(0 Stars)** Ans: 2 Crayons & 0 Stars	
9	5 = 3 + ? + ? 5 = 3 + **1** + **1**	**C**
10	4 = 9 - 2 - ? 4 = 7 - ? 4 = 7 - **3**	**E**
11	4 Wheels = ? + 1 Wheel + 1 Wheel 4 = ? + 1 + 1 4 = ? + 2 4 = **2** + 2 **(2 Wheels)** 4 Pencils = ? + 1 Pencil + 2 Pencils 4 = ? + 1 + 2 4 = ? + 3 4 = **1** + 3 **(1 Pencil)** Ans: 2 Wheels & 1 Pencil	**E**

12	5 Stars = 0 + 2 stars + ? 5 = 2 + ? 5 = 2 + **3** **(3 Stars)** 3 Pencils = 1 Pencil + 0 + ? 3 = 1 + ? 3 = 1 + **2** **(2 Pencils)** Ans: 3 Stars & 2 Pencils	**C**
13	9 = 4 + ? + 1 9 = 5 + ? 9 = 5 + **4**	**C**
14	5 = 9 - 7 + ? 5 = 2 + ? 5 = 2 + **3**	**A**
15	1 + 2 = 6 - ? 3 = 6 - ? 3 = 6 - **3**	**D**

NUMBER PUZZLES

in

NUMBER FORMAT

One-Step
Two-Step
&
Multi-Step
Equations

ADDITION

QUESTION		ANSWER
1	9 = 5 + ? 9 = 5 + 4	B
2	7 = 4 + ? 7 = 4 + 3	C
3	6 = ? + 6 6 = 0 + 6	B
4	8 = 2 + ? 8 = 2 + 6	A
5	3 = 1 + ? 3 = 1 + 2	E
6	5 = ? + 2 5 = 3 + 2	C
7	2 = 1 + ? 2 = 1 + 1	D
8	10 = 4 + ? 10 = 4 + 6	E
9	11 = ? + 7 11 = 4 + 7	A
10	15 = 5 + ? 15 = 5 + 10	B
11	12 = 8 + ? 12 = 8 + 4	A

12	6 = ? + 3 6 = 3 + 3	**C**
13	2 + 8 = 5 + ? 10 = 5 + ? 10 = 5 + 5	**A**
14	7 + 5 = 8 + ? 12 = 8 + ? 12 = 8 + 4	**A**
15	11 + 3 = ? + 8 14 = ? + 8 14 = 6 + 8	**B**
16	3 + 1 = ? + 0 4 = ? + 0 4 = 4 + 0	**B**
17	5 + ~~6~~ = ~~6~~ + ? 5 = ? 5 = 5	**B**
18	3 + 4 = ? + 5 7 = ? + 5 7 = 2 + 5	**E**
19	7 + 8 = 6 + ? 15 = 6 + ? 15 = 6 + 9	**E**

20	4 + 6 = 1 + ? 10 = 1 + ? 10 = 1 + 9	**B**
21	7 + 7 = ? + 9 14 = ? + 9 14 = 5 + 9	**D**
22	1 + 5 = 6 + ? ~~6~~ = ~~6~~ + ? 0 = ? 0 = 0	**C**
23	8 + 7 = 9 + ? 15 = 9 + ? 15 = 9 + 6	**E**
24	9 ~~+ 9~~ = ? + ~~9~~ 9 = ? 9 = 9	**B**
25	8 + 4 = 6 + 3 + ? 12 = 9 + ? 12 = 9 + 3	**A**
26	5 + 3 = 2 + ? + 2 8 = 4 + ? 8 = 4 + 4	**C**

27	6 + ~~9~~ = ? + ~~9~~ + 3 6 = ? + 3 6 = 3 + 3	**E**
28	8 + 5 = 3 + 1 + ? 13 = 4 + ? 13 = 4 + 9	**C**
29	3 + 5 = 8 + ? + 0 ~~8~~ = ~~8~~ + ? 0 = ? 0 = 0	**C**
30	9 + 9 = ? + 6 + 7 18 = ? + 13 18 = 5 + 13	**A**
31	7 + 3 = 1 + 1 + ? 10 = 2 + ? 10 = 2 + 8	**A**
32	2 + 6 = 4 + ? + 3 8 = 7 + ? 8 = 7 + 1	**B**
33	9 + 2 = ? + 8 + 1 ~~9~~ + 2 = ? + ~~9~~ 2 = ? 2 = 2	**C**

34	1 + 8 = 2 + 5 + ? 9 = 7 + ? 9 = 7 + 2	C
35	3 + 7 = 1 + ? + 2 10 = 3 + ? 10 = 3 + 7	C
36	9 + ~~7~~ = ? + 8 + ~~7~~ 9 = 8 + ? 9 = 8 + 1	A
37	~~2~~ + 3 + 4 = ~~2~~ + 1 + ? 7 = 1 + ? 7 = 1 + 6	B
38	5 + 3 + 4 = 6 + ? + 2 12 = 8 + ? 12 = 8 + 4	D
39	6 + 5 + ~~7~~ = ? + 10 + ~~7~~ 11 = ? + 10 11 = 1 + 10	A
40	1 + 8 + 2 = 9 + 1 + ? ~~9~~ + 2 = ~~9~~ + 1 + ? 2 = 1 + ? 2 = 1 + 1	E

41	7 + ~~3~~ + 1 = ~~3~~ + ? + 5 8 = ? + 5 8 = 3 + 5	**A**
42	5 + 5 + 5 = ? + 10 + 0 ~~10~~ + 5 = ? + ~~10~~ 5 = ? 5 = 5	**D**
43	6 + 6 + 1 = 5 + 5 + ? 13 = 10 + ? 13 = 10 + 3	**A**
44	1 + 9 + 3 = 11 + ? + 2 13 = 13 + ? 13 = 13 + 0	**A**
45	2 + 4 + 6 = ? + 8 + 1 12 = ? + 9 12 = 3 + 9	**E**
46	~~1~~ + 3 + ~~2~~ = ~~2~~ + ~~1~~ + ? 3 = ? 3 = 3	**A**
47	7 + 7 + 7 = 6 + ? + 8 21 = 14 + ? 21 = 14 + 7	**C**

48	3 + 7 + 0 = ? + 10 + 0 ~~10~~ = ? + ~~10~~ 0 = ? 0 = 0	**B**
49	7 + ? + 2 = 8 + 1 + 5 ~~9~~ + ? = ~~9~~ + 5 ? = 5 5 = 5	**E**
50	? + 4 + 6 = 6 + 0 + 9 ? + 10 = 15 5 + 10 = 15	**B**

One-Step
Two-Step
&
Multi-Step
Equations

SUBTRACTION

QUESTION		ANSWER
1	5 = 8 - ? 5 = 8 - 3	A
2	8 = 12 - ? 8 = 12 – 4	A
3	3 = 7 - ? 3 = 7 – 4	C
4	8 = 14 - ? 8 = 14 – 6	A
5	1 = 9 - ? 1 = 9 – 8	B
6	5 = ? - 2 5 = 7 – 2	D
7	2 = 6 - ? 2 = 6 – 4	B
8	1 = 4 - ? 1 = 4 - 3	C
9	2 = ? - 7 2 = 9 – 7	B
10	10 = 15 - ? 10 = 15 - 5	A
11	9 = 11 - ? 9 = 11 – 2	E

12	6 = ? - 3 6 = 9 - 3	C
13	2 + 4 = 12 - ? 6 = 12 - ? 6 = 12 - 6	B
14	3 + 5 = 9 - ? 8 = 9 - ? 8 = 9 – 1	D
15	1 + 3 = ? - 3 4 = ? - 3 4 = 7 – 3	E
16	3 + 1 = ? - 0 4 = ? - 0 4 = 4 – 0	B
17	5 + 2 = 10 - ? 7 = 10 - ? 7 = 10 – 3	A
18	3 + 4 = ? - 1 7 = ? - 1 7 = 8 – 1	A
19	8 - 7 = 6 - ? 1 = 6 - ? 1 = 6 - 5	D

20	7 - 2 = 8 - ? 5 = 8 - ? 5 = 8 - 3	A
21	9 - 7 = ? - 1 2 = ? - 1 2 = 3 – 1	C
22	5 - 1 = 8 - ? 4 = 8 - ? 4 = 8 – 4	B
23	8 - 5 = 9 - ? 3 = 9 - ? 3 = 9 – 6	E
24	9 - ~~9~~ = ? - ~~9~~ 9 = ? 9 = 9	B
25	4 + 2 = 9 – 1 - ? 6 = 8 - ? 6 = 8 – 2	E
26	5 + 3 = 10 + ? - 2 ~~8~~ = ~~8~~ + ? 0 = ? 0 = 0	B

27	2 + 5 = ? + 9 - 3 7 = ? + 6 7 = 1 + 6	**C**
28	4 + 1 = 11 + 1 - ? 5 = 12 - ? 5 = 12 – 7	**B**
29	2 + 2 = 8 - ? - 0 4 = 8 - ? 4 = 8 – 4	**D**
30	5 + 1 = ? - 1 - 1 6 = ? - 2 6 = 8 – 2	**A**
31	7 - 3 = 10 - 5 - ? 4 = 5 - ? 4 = 5 – 1	**A**
32	9 - 6 = 8 - ? - 3 3 = 5 - ? 3 = 5 – 2	**E**
33	8 - ~~2~~ = ? - ~~2~~ - 1 8 = ? - 1 8 = 9 – 1	**B**

34	1 + ~~1~~ = 8 + ~~1~~ - ? 1 = 8 - ? 1 = 8 – 7	C
35	3 + 8 = 9 + ? - 2 11 = 7 + ? 11 = 7 + 4	C
36	2 + 5 = ? + 1 - 1 7 = ? + 0 7 = 7 + 0	A
37	2 + 3 - 4 = 5 - 1 - ? 1 = 4 - ? 1 = 4 – 3	A
38	5 + 3 - 4 = 6 - ? - 2 4 = 4 - ? 4 = 4 – 0	E
39	6 - 5 + ~~1~~ = ? - 1 + ~~1~~ 1 = ? - 1 1 = 2 – 1	C
40	1 + 8 - 2 = 9 - 5 + ? 7 = 4 + ? 7 = 4 + 3	A

41	7 + 2 - 9 = 3 - ? - 1 0 = 2 - ? 0 = 2 – 2	C
42	5 + 5 - 5 = ? + 4 - 3 5 = ? + 1 5 = 4 + 1	B
43	6 - 6 + 1 = 5 + 5 - ? 1 = 10 - ? 1 = 10 – 9	D
44	9 - 5 + 3 = 11 + ? - 6 7 = 5 + ? 7 = 5 + 2	C
45	7 - 4 + 2 = ? + 8 - 3 5 = ? + 5 5 = 0 + 5	E
46	7 - 6 + ~~1~~ = 2 ~~+ 1~~ - ? 1 = 2 - ? 1 = 2 – 1	B
47	7 - 5 + 0 = 9 + ? - 8 2 = 1 + ? 2 = 1 + 1	C

48	9 - ~~8~~ + 1 = ? + 10 - ~~8~~ 10 = ? + 10 10 = 0 + 10	**B**
49	7 - ? + ~~2~~ = 8 -3 + ~~2~~ 7 - ? = 5 7 - 2 = 5	**C**
50	? - 4 + 6 = 6 - 0 + 3 ? + 2 = 9 7 + 2 = 9	**C**

One-Step Two-Step & Multi-Step Equations

DIVISION

QUESTION		ANSWER
1	8 = ? + ? 8 = 4 + 4	B
2	6 = ? + ? 6 = 3 + 3	C
3	4 = ? + ? 4 = 2 + 2	E
4	2 = ? + ? 2 = 1 + 1	D
5	10 = ? + ? 10 = 5 + 5	B
6	12 = ? + ? 12 = 6 + 6	C
7	20 = ? + ? 20 = 10 + 10	B
8	14 = ? + ? 14 = 7 + 7	C
9	16 = ? + ? 16 = 8 + 8	D
10	2 = ? + ? 2 = 1 + 1	B
11	12 = ? + ? 12 = 6 + 6	E
12	10 = ? + ?	D

	10 = 5 + 5	
13	2 + 6 = ? + ? 8 = ? + ? 8 = 4 + 4	E
14	7 + 5 = ? + ? 12 = ? + ? 12 = 6 + 6	E
15	11 + 3 = ? + ? 14 = ? + ? 14 = 7 + 7	C
16	3 + 1 = ? + ? 4 = ? + ? 4 = 2 + 2	C
17	4 + 6 = ? + ? 10 = ? + ? 10 = 5 + 5	B
18	8 + 4 = ? + ? 12 = ? + ? 12 = 6 + 6	C
19	7 + 5 = 6 + ? + ? 12 = 6 + ? + ? 12 = 6 + 3 + 3	D
20	4 + 5 = 1 + ? + ?	C

	9 = 1 + ? + ? 9 = 1 + 4 + 4	
21	7 + 9 = ? + 6 + ? 16 = ? + 6 + ? 16 = 5 + 6 + 5	D
22	1 + 5 = 6 + ? + ? 6 = 6 + ? + ? 6 = 6 + 0 + 0	C
23	~~3~~ + 8 = ? + ~~3~~ + ? 8 = ? + ? 8 = 4 + 4	E
24	10 + ~~9~~ = ? + ~~9~~ + ? 10 = ? + ? 10 = 5 + 5	B
25	8 + 4 = ? + ? + ? 12 = ? + ? + ? 12 = 4 + 4 + 4	B
26	5 + 4 = ? + ? + ? 9 = ? + ? + ? 9 = 3 + 3 + 3	A
27	6 + 9 = ? + ? + ?	A

	15 = ? + ? + ? 15 = 5 + 5 + 5	
28	9 + 9 = ? + ? + ? 18 = ? + ? + ? 18 = 6 + 6 + 6	D
29	2 + 1 = ? + ? + ? 3 = ? + ? + ? 3 = 1 + 1 + 1	B
30	1 + 5 = ? + ? + ? 6 = ? + ? + ? 6 = 2 + 2 + 2	B
31	7 + 3 = ? + 2 + ? 10 = ? + 2 + ? 10 = 4 + 2 + 4	D
32	2 + 6 = ? + ? + 4 8 = ? + ? + 4 8 = 2 + 2 + 4	E
33	9 + 3 = ? + ? + 4 12 = ? + ? + 4 12 = 4 + 4 + 4	B
34	5 + 9 = ? + 8 + ?	A

	14 = ? + 8 + ? 14 = 3 + 8 + 3	
35	3 + 5 = 6 + ? + ? 8 = 6 + ? + ? 8 = 6 + 1 + 1	**C**
36	9 + 7 = ? + ? + 8 16 = ? + ? + 8 16 = 4 + 4 + 8	**B**
37	2 + 9 + 4 = ? + 5 + ? 15 = ? + 5 + ? 15 = 5 + 5 + 5	**E**
38	~~5~~ + 4 + 4 = ? + ? + ~~5~~ 8 = ? + ? 8 = 4 + 4	**D**
39	4 + 5 + 6 = ? + 9 + ? 15 = ? + 9 + ? 15 = 3 + 9 + 3	**E**
40	3 + ~~8~~ + 7 = ~~8~~ + ? + ? 10 = ? + ? 10 = 5 + 5	**C**
41	1 + 3 + 2 = ? + ? + 4	**B**

	6 = ? + ? + 4 6 = 1 + 1 + 4	
42	5 + ~~8~~ + 7 = ? + ? + ~~8~~ 12 = ? + ? 12 = 6 + 6	**C**
43	6 + 6 + 8 = ? + 12 + ? ~~12~~ + 8 = ? + ~~12~~ + ? 8 = ? + ? 8 = 4 + 4	**D**
44	1 + 9 + 3 = 7 + ? + ? 13 = 7 + ? + ? 13 = 7 + 3 + 3	**D**
45	5 + 4 + 6 = ? + ? + 9 ~~9~~ + 6 = ? + ? + ~~9~~ 6 = ? + ? 6 = 3 + 3	**E**
46	1 + 7 + 5 = ? + 9 + ? 13 = ? + 9 + ? 13 = 2 + 9 + 2	**C**
47	7 + 7 + 7 = ? + ? + 11 21 = ? + ? + 11 21 = 5 + 5 + 11	**B**
48	0 + 7 + 0 = ? + ? + 1	**E**

	7 = ? + ? + 1 7 = 3 + 3 + 1	
49	5 + 0 + 4 = ? + ? + ? 9 = ? + ? + ? 9 = 3 + 3 + 3	**A**
50	0 + ~~4~~ + 6 = ? + ~~4~~ + ? 6 = ? + ? 6 = 3 + 3	**A**